COMPACT
Aktives Lernen

ENGLISH IDIOMS
schnell kapiert

Susan Bollinger

Compact Verlag

© 2000 Compact Verlag München

Redaktion: Friedrich Rojahn, Bea Herrmann, Karina Partsch
Redaktionsassistenz: Katharina Eska, Johanna Kappelmann
Illustrationen: Atelier Andreas Piel
Produktionsleitung: Uwe Eckhard
Umschlaggestaltung: Inga Koch

Besuchen Sie uns im Internet: www.compactverlag.de

ISBN 3-8174-7139-4
7371391

Einleitung

Eine Fremdsprache richtig zu beherrschen heißt, auch die Idiomatik der Sprache im Griff zu haben. Besonders im Englischen werden im täglichen Sprachgebrauch viele Redewendungen und Sprichwörter verwendet, die sich nicht einfach durch eine wörtliche Übersetzung oder das Nachschlagen in einem Wörterbuch erklären lassen.

Um solche Redewendungen geht es in „Englisch Idioms – schnell kapiert". In alphabetischer Reihenfolge wird eine Vielzahl typischer Redewendungen und Sprichwörter vorgestellt. Jeder Begriff wird entweder übersetzt oder erklärt. Zudem wird in vielen Fällen durch Beispielsätze die Verwendung im alltäglichen Sprachgebrauch verdeutlicht. Die gebräuchlichsten Idiome sind zur besseren Einprägsamkeit farblich markiert. Ein Register deutscher Sprichwörter ermöglicht einen schnellen Zugriff auf bestimmte englische Redewendungen über die deutsche Sprache.

Soweit nicht anders ausgewiesen, sind die Redewendungen sowohl im amerikanischen wie im britischen Englisch geläufig. Slangausdrücke sind als solche gekennzeichnet und wurden der Alltagssprache entnommen.

Als praktisches und zuverlässiges Nachschlagewerk ist „English Idioms – schnell kapiert" der ideale Begleiter für alle, die ein flüssiges und idiomatisch richtiges Englisch sprechen möchten.

A

able:
~ to breathe (easily/freely) again — aufatmen können
~ to do something blindfold(ed)/ — etwas mit links erledigen/
~ to do something standing on one's head — etwas im Schlaf erledigen
~ to take a joke — einen Spaß verstehen (können)
~ to take something — etwas aushalten können

about:
be ~ to do s.th. — drauf und dran sein, etwas zu tun
up and ~ — wieder auf den Beinen

above:
~ all — vor allem
~ board — offen, ehrlich
get ~ oneself — eingebildet sein, sich überschätzen
not to be ~ doing s.th. — sich nicht zu fein sein, etwas zu tun

accident:
by ~ — zufällig
meet with an ~ — verunglücken

accord:
of one's own ~ — aus eigenem Antrieb, von selbst, von sich aus
with one ~ — einstimmig
~ing to all accounts — alle behaupten; laut Berichten/Aussagen
~ing to s.o. or s.th. — laut ...

account:
~ account for — erklären
of no ~ — bedeutungslos

act upon/on — aufgrund von etwas handeln

add up to s.th. — 1. eine mathematische Summe bilden, 2. bedeuten

1. *The shopping adds up to almost a hundred pounds.*
2. *I don't see what all this adds up to. What do you mean?*

advantage:
to have the ~ of — den Vorteil haben
to take ~ of — 1. jdn. ausnutzen 2. eine Gelegenheit nutzen

1. *The car dealer took advantage of his customer's gullibility.*
2. *I took advantage of the fine weather to play tennis.*

after:
~ all — schließlich, letztendlich, doch
~ hours — nach Büro- oder Ladenschluss
be ~ s.o. — jdm. oder etwas hinterherjagen

again:
now and ~ — ab und zu
time and ~ — immer wieder

against:
~ the clock — im Wettlauf mit der Zeit
~ the grain — gegen den Strich
as ~ him — im Vergleich zu ihm

age:
act one's ~ — nicht albern sein, sich benehmen
be of ~ — volljährig sein
come of ~ — volljährig werden
for ~s — seit langer Zeit

agree:
~ with s.o. or s.th. — die Meinung von jdm. teilen
not ~ with s.o. — jdm. nicht bekommen, krank machen

Travelling by boat does not agree with me, it always makes me feel sick.

ahead:
~ of time — vorher, vor der angekündigten Zeit, früher
get ~ — Karriere machen

air:
in the ~ — 1. ungewiss, 2. in der Luft liegen
1. *We go to Paris tomorrow, but after that our plans are in the air.*
2. *There are rumours in the air of a strike at the factory.*

give o.s. ~s — sich zieren, vornehm tun
~s and graces — Allüren

alive:
~ and kicking — lebendig, aktiv
~ with — wimmeln von, voll sein von
The river was alive with fish.

all:
~ alone — ganz allein
~ along — die ganze Zeit
~ the best — viel Glück!
~ right — in Ordnung
~ the same — dennoch, trotzdem
for ~ I care — meinetwegen
not at ~ — überhaupt nicht
~ but — beinahe, fast
to be ~ ears — ganz Ohr sein
on ~ fours — auf allen vieren
~ in all — alles in allem
~ in one piece — sicher, unversehrt, heil
~ out — mit Volldampf
~ over — 1. überall, 2. vorbei, 3. typisch für
1. *There were celebrations all over town.*
2. *They did not leave until the excitement was all over.*
3. *John handed in his essay late, but that's John all over.*

~ the same — 1. gleich, 2. trotzdem
1. *It's all the same to me.*
2. *All the same, I think you're wrong.*

for ~ that — trotzdem
when ~'s said and done — unterm Strich
not ~ there (Sl.) — nicht ganz bei Trost
~ thumbs — zwei linke Hände, ungeschickt
~'s well that ends well. (Sprichw.) — Ende gut, alles gut!
~ year round — das ganze Jahr über/hindurch

allow:
~ for s.o. or s.th.	in Betracht ziehen, berücksichtigen
~ of no argument	keinen Einwand zulassen, keinen Widerspruch dulden

along:
~ with	zusammen mit, in Gesellschaft von
be ~ in a minute	gleich kommen
go ~ with (Sl.)	zustimmen, mitmachen

answer:
~ back	frech werden, widersprechen
~ for	die Verantwortung übernehmen
~ a purpose	geeignet sein, einen Zweck erfüllen
~ to s.o.	sich jemandem gegenüber rechtfertigen
~ (to)	1. übereinstimmen, entsprechen, 2. hören auf

1. A man answering (to) that description was seen leaving the bank.
2. He answers to the name of John Doe.

appearances:
to all ~	offensichtlich, anscheinend
keep up ~	den Schein wahren

apple:
be the ~ of s.o.'s eye	jdm. besonders wert/lieb sein

arm:
~ o.s. against	sich gegen etwas wappnen
~ o.s. with s.th.	sich mit etwas bewaffnen
armed to the teeth (Sl.)	bis an die Zähne bewaffnet
keep s.b. at ~'s length	jdn. auf Distanz halten
within ~'s reach	in Reichweite

as:
~ for you	was dich betrifft
~ it were	sozusagen
~ yet	bis jetzt
I thought ~ much	Das hab' ich mir gedacht.
~ the case stands	wie die Dinge stehen
~ a rule	in der Regel
~ a last resort	als Letztes, wenn alles andere schief geht

~ **a matter of course**	selbstverständlich, an der Tagesordnung
~ **a matter of fact**	im Übrigen

As a matter of fact, I saw him yesterday.

~ **blind** ~ **a bat**	sehr kurzsichtig

*I'm getting as blind as bat,
I must get some spectacles.*

~ **busy** ~ **a bee**	eifrig, sehr beschäftigt

~ **clear** ~ **mud** (Sl.)	sehr unverständlich

*I'm afraid I can't see the point at all,
your argument is as clear as mud.*

~ **cool** ~ **a cucumber**	beherrscht, ruhig

*She never loses her temper,
she's as cool as a cucumber.*

~ **easy** ~ **pie** (Sl.)	babyleicht
~ **far** ~ **I'm concerned**	was mich betrifft
~ **fit** ~ **a fiddle** (Sl.)	kerngesund

The doctor told me I'm as fit as a fiddle.

~ **good** ~ **done**	beinahe fertig/erledigt
~ **happy** ~ **a lark**	glücklich und zufrieden
~ **hard** ~ **nails**	kalt und grausam
~ **light** ~ **a feather**	federleicht
~ **mad** ~ **a March hare**	total verrückt
~ **mad** ~ **hell** (Sl.)	wütend
~ **quick** ~ **a wink**	sehr schnell
~ **regular** ~ **clockwork**	pünktlich wie die Uhr
~ **sick** ~ **a dog**	sehr schlecht, übel, speiübel
~ **smart** ~ **a fox**	sehr schlau
~ **snug** ~ **a bug in a rug** (Sl.)	warm, geborgen, sicher

The mother tucked her daughter up in be and said: "There you are, as snug as a bug in a rug".

~ **thick** ~ **thieves**	unzertrennlich, wie Pech und Schwefel
~ **tough** ~ **old boots**	zäh wie Leder
~ **wise** ~ **an owl**	sehr weise

ask:
~ **for the moon**	zu viel/das Unmögliche verlangen
~ **for trouble**	Schwierigkeiten heraufbeschwören

at:
~ **all costs**	um jeden Preis
~ **all times**	ständig, immer

I have said it again and again, you have to tell me the truth at all times.

~ **any rate**	auf jeden Fall
~ **every turn**	überall (wo man hinschaut)

The playful kitten gets under my feet at every turn.

~ **first**	am Anfang, zuerst
~ **hand**	griffbereit
~ **length**	ausführlich
be ~ **loggerheads**	im Streit, sich in den Haaren liegen

The two brothers were always at loggerheads, they could never agree.

~ **long last**	endlich
~ **a loose end**	rastlos, ziellos, unruhig, ohne Arbeit

John was at a loose end and was glad to join me for an evening in the cinema.

(lost) ~ **sea**	durcheinander, konfus
~ **odds with s.o.**	im Streit

Don't pay attention to him, he's at odds with everyone today.

~ **one fell swoop**	plötzlich, auf einmal
~ **one's wits end**	mit seiner Weisheit am Ende

I'm at my wits end. What shall I do?

~ **short notice**	kurzfristig

It is not easy to get an appointment with the dentist at short notice.

~ **the crack of dawn**	bei Tagesanbruch, sehr früh
~ **the drop of a hat**	im Nu
~ **the end of one's tether**	fix und fertig
~ **the eleventh hour**	fünf vor zwölf
~ **will**	wann immer man will

avenge:
~ o.s. on s.b. for s.th. — sich für etwas an jdm. rächen

aware:
make s.b. ~ of s.th. — jdm. etwas klar, bewusst machen

away:
~ with that! — Weg damit!
right ~ — jetzt gleich, sofort

B

back:
~ and forth — hin und her
bend over ~wards — sich übergroße Mühe geben
get off s.o.'s ~ — jdn. in Ruhe lassen
~stairs — indirekt, nicht offiziell
You should not listen to backstairs gossip.
go ~ on one's word — sein Wort brechen
go ~ on s.o. — jdn. im Stich lassen
hang ~ — zurück bleiben, sich im Hintergrund halten
with one's ~ to the wall — in die Enge getrieben

bad:
~ form — schlechter Stil, unhöflich
want s.th. ~ly — etwas dringend brauchen, unbedingt haben wollen

bag:
in the ~ — unter Dach und Fach
~ and baggage — mit Kind und Kegel

balance:
to hold the ~ — das Zünglein an der Waage bilden
on ~ — wenn man alles bedenkt
strike a ~ — Bilanz ziehen

ball:
be on the ~ — am Ball sein
have a ~ — einen Mordsspaß haben
The ~'s in your court. — Jetzt sind Sie dran!

bare:
~ one's heart — sein Herz ausschütten
~ one's teeth — die Zähne zeigen

bargain:
~ for — rechnen mit
We didn't bargain for so many people coming to the party.
into the ~ — hinzu
make the best of a bad ~ — das Beste draus machen
strike a ~ — einen Kompromiss schließen

bark:
His ~ is worse than his bite. — Hunde, die bellen, beißen nicht.
~ up the wrong tree — falsch liegen

bat:
like a ~ out of hell (engl./Sl.) — wie ein geölter Blitz
He was so frightened he ran out of the house like a bat out of hell.
have ~s in the belfry (Sl.) — einen Vogel haben
off one's own ~ — ohne Hilfe, aus eigener Initiative, von sich aus

be:
that's the ~ all and end all — das ist das A und O
for the time ~ing — zunächst, im Moment
~ a must (Sl.) — etwas, das man tun muss; es gehört dazu, ein Muss sein

~ **all ears**   ganz Ohr sein
Do tell me your story. I'm all ears!
~ **poles apart**   da liegen Welten dazwischen
~ **beside oneself with joy**   vor Freude ganz aus dem Häuschen sein
~ **that as it may**   trotzdem
~ **the spitting image of s.o.** (Sl.)   jdm. wie aus dem Gesicht geschnitten sein
He is the spitting image of his brother, it is hard to tell them apart.
~ **full of beans**   springlebendig sein

bear:
~ **up**   durchhalten, standhalten
s.th. ~s watching   etwas muss im Auge behalten werden

Our situation is critical and will bear watching.
~ **in mind**   etwas nicht vergessen
Bear what I have said in mind when you go for the interview.

beat:
~ **about the bush**   um den heißen Brei herum reden
Stop beating about the bush and come to the point.
~ **a retreat**   fliehen
becoming to s.o.   jdm. gut stehen
You should always wear that dress, it is very becoming to you.

a bee in one's bonnet
He has a bee in his bonnet about changing the world.

fixe Idee

before:
~ long
~ you know it
carry all ~ one

bald, binnen kurzem
bevor man sich versieht
gelingen in allem, was man anfängt

beg to differ

anderer Meinung sein

behave like a bull in a china shop

sich wie ein Elefant im Porzellanladen benehmen

behind one's back

hinter dem Rücken von jdm.

bend:
~ over backwards to do s.th.

sich übermäßig anstrengen, etwas zu tun

round the ~

nicht alle Tassen im Schrank haben, verrückt sein

best:
at the ~ of times
be all for the ~
get the ~ of s.o.
to the ~ of my knowledge
put the ~ foot forward

bestenfalls
zum Besten von jdm. sein
jdn. übers Ohr hauen
so viel ich weiß
so schnell wie möglich gehen

between:
in ~
~ ourselves
read ~ the lines
~ the devil and the deep blue sea (Sl.)
He couldn't make up his mind as to what to decide. He was obviously between devil and the deep blue sea.

mittendrin, dazwischen
unter uns
zwischen den Zeilen lesen
in der Klemme

beyond:
That's ~ me.
live ~ one's means
~ (all) bearing

Das ist mir zu hoch.
über seine Verhältnisse leben
unerträglich

bird:
The early ~ catches the worm. (Sprichw.)

Morgenstund hat Gold im Mund.

A ~ in the hand is worth two in the bush. (Sprichw.)

Ein Spatz in der Hand ist besser als eine Taube auf dem Dach.

~s of a feather flock together. (Sprichw.)

Gleich und Gleich gesellt sich gern.

kill two ~s with one stone (Sl.)

zwei Fliegen mit einer Klappe schlagen

When you go to the chemist's for your prescription, you could bring me my medicine, that would be killing two birds with one stone.

bite:
~ **back a remark**
~ **off more than one can chew**
~ **the dust**
~ **the hand that feeds you**

sich eine Bemerkung verkneifen
sich zu viel zumuten
ins Gras beißen
den Ast absägen, auf dem man sitzt

What's bitten him?

Was ist mit ihm los?

black:
~ **out**

umkippen, das Bewusstsein verlieren

not so ~ as one is painted

nicht so schlecht wie die Leute sagen

~ **sheep of the family**

das schwarze Schaf der Familie

in ~ and white — schwarz auf weiß

in the blink of an eye — urplötzlich, blitzschnell

blind:
a ~ alley — ein Sackgasse
turn a ~ eye — ein Auge zudrücken

blood:
~ is thicker than water. — Blut ist dicker als Wasser.
bad ~ — böses Blut
There has been bad blood between Zoe and her sister for ages.
blue-~ — adelig
in cold ~ — kaltblütig
The judge said the murderer had acted in cold blood, and therefore deserved the hardest punishment provided for by law.

blot one's copy book — sich etwas zu Schulden kommen lassen

blow:
~ one's top (Sl.) — vor Wut explodieren
If you irritate him much more he'll blow his top.
~ off steam — Dampf ablassen
Jack was so angry after the meeting, he just had to blow off steam.
~ hot and cold — sein Fähnchen nach dem Wind drehen
~ one's own trumpet — sich selber loben
She is not a modest person at all, she's always blowing her own trumpet.
~ over — vorübergehen, aufhören
We often have a row, but they soon blow over.

blue:
feel ~ — deprimiert sein
~ murder — eine heftige Szene
There'll be blue murder when she hears of this.

like a bolt from the ~	wie ein Blitz aus heiterem Himmel
His news came as a complete surprise, like a bolt from the blue.	
once in a ~ moon	äußerst selten, alle Jubeljahre
it boils down to	es läuft darauf hinaus, dass

bone:
have a ~ to pick with s.b.	mit jdm. ein Hühnchen zu rupfen haben
make not ~s about s.th.	keinen Hehl daraus machen
~ of contention	Zankapfel, Streitobjekt

book:
in my ~	so wie ich die Sache sehe, was mich betrifft
suit s.b.'s ~	jdm. in den Kram passen
The arrangement will suit my book very well.	
go by the ~	sich genau an die Regeln halten
It's a closed ~ to me.	Das ist ein Buch mit sieben Siegeln für mich.

boot:
My heart is in my ~s.	Das Herz ist mir in die Hose gerutscht.
The ~ is on the other foot.	Die Sache ist gerade umgekehrt.
~ s.o. out	jdn. hinausschmeißen

born:
~ with a silver spoon in one's mouth (Sl.) — ein Glückskind sein
She has never had to worry about money, she was born with a silver spoon in her mouth.
I was not ~ yesterday. (Sl.) — Ich bin nicht von gestern.

bread and butter — Einkommen, Lebensunterhalt
I hate being a mechanic, but it's my bread and butter.

break:
~ away from — Abstand nehmen von
~ down s.th. — 1. etwas gewaltsam zerstören, 2. etwas überwinden, 3. zusammenbrechen

1. *The police had to break down the door in order to get into the apartment.*
2. *It took a long time to break down his inhibitions.*
3. *After the accident, she broke down completely.*

~ new ground — etwas völlig Neues machen, Neuland betreten

~-through — ein (revolutionärer) Durchbruch

make a clean breast (of) — offen etwas eingestehen

breath:
a ~ of fresh air — neu, frisch, fantasievoll
She has a wonderful personality, just like a breath of fresh air.
under one's ~ — leise, geflüstert, still
He went away swearing under his breath.

brick:
come down like a ton of ~s — jdn. aufs Heftigste kritisieren
The manager came down like a ton of bricks on him for losing the money.
drop a ~(Sl.) — einen Schnitzer machen

bring:
~ about — zustande bringen
~ about a change — eine Änderung mit sich bringen

~ **into play**	ins Spiel bringen
~ **o.s. to**	sich überwinden
She couldn't bring herself to apologize.	
~ **out**	zum Vorschein bringen
The crisis brought out the best in him.	
~ **s.b. down**	jdn. zur Strecke bringen
~ **s.b. down to earth**	jdn. auf den Boden der Tatsachen zurückholen
~ **s.b. in one s.th.**	jdn. an etwas teil haben lassen
~ **s.th. home to s.b.**	jdn. etwas klarmachen, erklären
~ **s.th. into the open**	etwas ans Tageslicht bringen
~ **s.b. to his senses**	jdn. zur Vernunft bringen
~ **s.th. to a close**	beenden, zu Ende bringen
~ **s.th. to light**	etwas aufdecken, ans Tageslicht bringen
~ **the house down**	Zuschauer zu begeistertem Applaus hinreißen

broad:
It's about as ~ as it's long	das ist gehupft wie gesprungen
~ly speaking	allgemein gesprochen

Buck up! (Sl.)	Kopf hoch!

build:
~ **one's hopes on**	seine Hoffnungen auf etwas setzen
~ **castles in the air**	Luftschlösser bauen
I like to sit in my chair just building castles in the air.	

bull:
like a ~ in a china shop	wie ein Elefant im Porzellanladen
go like a ~ at a gate	mit der Tür ins Haus fallen

bump:
~ **s.b. off** (Sl.)	jdn. um die Ecke bringen/töten
~ **into s.b.**	jdm. zufällig begegnen

burn:
~ **one's bridges behind one**	alle Brücken hinter sich abbrechen
If you leave university now you'll be burning your bridges behind you.	

~ one's boats	alle Brücken hinter sich abbrechen
~ the candle at boths ends	sich Tag und Nacht keine Ruhe gönnen
~ the midnight oil (Sl.)	bis spät in die Nacht arbeiten/aufbleiben

business:
That's none of your ~.   Das geht dich nichts an.
Mind your own ~.   Kümmere dich um deine eigenen Angelegenheiten.

but:
I cannot ~ (help him)   ich kann nicht anders (als ihm helfen)
the next ~ one   der übernächste
No ifs and ~s!   Keine Widerrede!

have butterflies in one's stomach   nervös sein
I am really nervous about the interview, I have butterflies in my stomach.

buy:
~ s.th. for a song   etwas ganz billig erstehen
~ s.b. off   jdn. abfinden
I'm determined to have my rights. I'll not let them buy me off.

by:

~ **and** ~	allmählich, nach und nach
~ **chance**	zufällig
~ **a hair's breadth**	knapp, um Haaresbreite

The athlete just missed breaking the record by a hair's breadth.

~ **all means**	in jedem Fall
~ **and large**	(für) gewöhnlich, im Allgemeinen
~ **hook or** ~ **cook** (Sl.)	auf Biegen und Brechen
~ **no means**	auf keinen Fall
~ **the dozens**	zu Dutzenden

The fans flocked to the concert by the dozens.

~ **the scruff of the neck**	am Kragen

He grabbed me by the scruff of the neck and threatened to hit me.

~ **the skin of one's teeth** (Sl.)	gerade, knapp

I just managed to catch the bus, by the skin of my teeth.

~ **the sweat of one's brow**	im Schweiße meines Angesichts
~ **the way**	im Übrigen

C

cake:

like hot ~**s**	wie warme Semmeln, sehr schnell

His latest book is selling like hot cakes.

a piece of ~ (Sl.)	einfach, leicht

He pretended that going into the lion's cage was a piece of cake.

call:

~ **at s.b.'s house**	bei jdm. vorbeischauen
~ **for s.b.**	nach jdm. rufen, jdn. abholen
~ **off s.th.**	etwas abblasen

We were going to go to the disco, but decided to call it off.

~ **on s.b.**	jdn. besuchen
~ **s.b. names**	jdn. beschimpfen
~ **it a day**	Feierabend machen

~ **to mind**	ins Gedächtnis rufen
~ **the tune**	die Entscheidung treffen
to give s.o. a ~	jdn. anrufen, sich bei jdm. melden

candle:
be not worth the ~	nicht der Mühe wert sein
burn the ~ at both ends	sich überarbeiten, überanstrengen

Poor Gary is completely worn out, he has been burning the candle at both ends lately.

not fit to hold a ~ to s.o.	jdm. nicht das Wasser reichen können

can't:
one ~ see one's hand in front of one's face	die Hand nicht vor den Augen sehen können
I ~ stand it.	Ich halte es nicht aus. Ich kann es nicht ausstehen.

cap:
put on one's thinking-~	über ein Problem nachdenken

There must be an answer to the problem, I must put on my thinking-cap.

If the ~ fits (wear it).	Wenn man sich betroffen fühlt, muss man entsprechend handeln.

I don't care.	Das ist mir egal. Meinetwegen.

carry:
~ **coals to Newcastle** (engl.)	Eulen nach Athen tragen
~ **all before one**	sehr erfolgreich sein
~ **the day**	Sieger sein
~ **the point**	jdn. überzeugen
~ **on**	1. sich aufführen, 2. weitermachen

1. *Jane, stop carrying on like that, you ought to be ashamed of yourself.*
2. *Carry on, you're doing just fine!*

~ **a torch for s.o.**	jdn. lieben, ohne geliebt zu werden
~ **the torch**	für eine Sache kämpfen
~ **weight**	wichtig sein, beeinflussen

There's no need to worry about John. What he says carries no weight.

put the cart before the horse	das Pferd am Schwanz aufzäumen

case:
in any ~   wie dem auch sei, in jedem Fall
in ~   im Falle, dass; falls
just in ~   für alle Fälle; nur für den Fall, dass

be out of cash   nicht gut bei Kasse sein

cat:
have a ~ nap   ein Nickerchen machen
let the ~ out of the bag   ein Geheimnis lüften, die Katze aus dem Sack lassen
put the ~ among the pigeons   Unruhe stiften, für Aufregung sorgen, Wirbel machen
wait for the ~ to jump   abwarten, wie sich der Gegner verhält

catch:
~ a straw   nach jedem Strohhalm greifen
~ one's death of cold   sich den Tod holen (erkälten)
~ s.o. red-handed   jdn. in flagranti erwischen
~ s.o.'s eye   die Aufmerksamkeit auf sich lenken
~ one's breath   wieder zu Atem kommen
~ on   Mode werden
~ sight of s.th.   etwas erblicken

certain:
make ~   sich vergewissern
That's for ~.   Das ist sicher.

chalk:
~ up — 1. anrechnen, 2. anschreiben lassen
as like as ~ and cheese — einander gleichen wie Tag und Nacht

The brothers are about as alike as chalk and cheese.

chance:
~ upon s.th./s.o. — etwas/jdn. zufällig finden
He never takes a ~. — Er geht nie ein Risiko ein.
stand a fair ~ — eine gute Chance haben

change:
~ hands — den Besitzer wechseln
That shop only ever changed hands once.
~ one's mind — es sich anders überlegen, die Meinung ändern
~ one's tune — die Einstellung/den Ton ändern, kleinlaut werden

You still soon change your tune when your hear what is in store for you.

charge:
be in ~ of — der Chef sein, die Verantwortung haben
free of ~ — kostenlos
~ s.th. to s.o. or s.th. — etwas auf Rechnung anderer kaufen

She charged her new car to her father.

Charity begins at home. (Sprichw.) — Jeder ist sich selbst der Nächste.

cheer:
~ s.o. up — jdn. aufheitern
~ up — Kopf hoch

chest:
get s.th. off one's ~ (engl.) — reinen Tisch machen
Thank goodness I've told you. I've been wanting to get that off my chest for a long time.

chew over s.th. (Sl.) — etwas diskutieren, über etwas nachdenken

chicken:
~-feed (am./Sl.) wertlos, vernachlässigbar
The cost will be chicken-feed
in comparison to the gains.
~ out of s.th. (Sl.) einen Rückzieher machen, abhauen
It's no good trying to chicken out now,
you have agreed to the plan.
count one's ~ before they're den Tag vor dem Abend loben, sich
hatched zu früh freuen

be a chip off the old block (Sl.) Der Apfel fällt nicht weit vom Stamm.

chop and chance rein in die Kartoffeln, raus aus den Kartoffeln

clap:
~ eyes on (meistens negativ) zu Gesicht bekommen

~-trap Geschwätz

clean:
be ~ out of s.th. (am./Sl.) gerade eben ausverkauft
~ up sauber machen, aufräumen, großen Gewinn machen

John won at the races
and really cleaned up.
make a ~ sweep reinen Tisch machen

clear:
~ cut scharf umrissen, eindeutig

with a ~ conscience	mit gutem Gewissen
~ as crystal	ganz offensichtlich
~ off	weggehen, abhauen
~ the air	Missverständnisse aus dem Weg räumen
~ s.th. up	1. deutlich und klar machen, 2. aufräumen, 3. schöner werden (Wetter)

1. *I am trying to clear up the misunderstanding.*
2. *You'll have to clear up your room before you invite your friends.*
3. *The weather has cleared up, we can go for a walk.*

The coast is ~.	Die Luft ist rein.

clock:
It worked like ~work.	Es lief wie am Schnürchen.
work against the ~	gegen die Uhr arbeiten

close:
a ~d book	unverständlich, ein Rätsel

Physics is a closed book to me.

at ~ quarters	dicht dran, nahe
~ one's eyes to s.th.	die Augen vor etwas verschließen
~ in on	sich nähern und umzingeln
the days ~ in	die Tage werden kürzer
~ up shop (Sl.)	Feierabend machen

It's six o'clock, time to close up shop for today.

be ~ at hand	in der Nähe sein
That was a ~ shave! (Sl.)	Das ging glimpflich aus.

cloud:
in the ~s	in Gedanken
under a ~	mit angeschlagenem Ruf/Ansehen

live in clover	wie Gott in Frankreich leben

not have a clue	keine Ahnung haben

coin:
pay s.b. back in his own ~	es jdm. mit gleicher Münze heimzahlen
the other side of the ~	die Kehrseite der Medaille

cold:
in ~ blood kaltblütig, absichtlich
give s.b. the ~ shoulder jdm. die kalte Schulter zeigen
throw ~ water on s.th. die Begeisterung dämpfen

colour:
~ up rot werden
come through with flying ~s einen glänzenden Sieg erringen
have a high ~ rot im Gesicht sein
show one's true ~s Farbe bekennen
off ~ nicht ganz fit

come:
~ about sich ereignen
~ across 1. überqueren, 2. finden, zufällig treffen

1. He came across the road to greet me.
2. Tidying up my room, I came across a couple of old love letters.

~ along 1. mitkommen, 2. Beeil dich!
~ down with s.th. an etwas erkranken
John is coming down with the flu, he must go to bed.

~ **into line with**	übereinstimmen mit
~ **into the open**	offenbaren, mit etwas herausrücken

You must come into the open and say what you really think.

~ **round**	das Bewusstsein wiedererlangen
~ **to a bad end**	ein böses Ende nehmen
~ **to blows**	sich schlagen

The two brothers came to blows over the girl.

~ **to grief**	Pech/Unglück haben

He was learning to skate but came to grief at the corner.

~ **to nothing**	Es wird nichts daraus.
~ **to one's senses**	wieder zu sich kommen
~ **to s.b.'s help**	jdn. zu Hilfe kommen
~ **to the point**	zur Sache kommen
~ **to a head**	sich zuspitzen (Situation)
~ **up in the world**	es zu etwas bringen

Since I started my new job I've really come up in the world.

~ **up with s.th.**	etwas vorschlagen, sich etwas einfallen lassen

It was Joseph who came up with the idea of moving house.

~ **what may**	was auch immer geschieht
have s.th. in common with	etwas gemeinsam haben mit
fish for compliments	sich selbst schlecht machen, in der Hoffnung, Widerspruch zu ernten

Harriet said her cooking skills were fairly moderate; she was obviously fishing for compliments.

condition:

on ~ that	unter der Bedingung, dass

I'll come, on condition that I receive a proper invitation.

out of ~	in schlechter Verfassung

cook:

~ **the books** (engl.)	Bücher fälschen
~ **s.o.'s goose**	jdn. ins Verderben stürzen

That's the way the cookie crumbles. (am./Sl.) Das ist der Lauf der Welt.

cool:
~ **customer** (Sl.) ein souveräner Typ, gerissener Kerl
~ **it!** (am./Sl.)/**Keep** ~**!** (engl./Sl.) Beruhige dich!
~ **down** abkühlen, sich beruhigen

cost:
at all ~**s** um jeden Preis
~ **a packet** (am./Sl.) extrem teuer

count:
~ **against s.th.** gegen etwas sprechen
lose ~ **of** sich verzählen, den Überblick verlieren
~ **on s.b** auf jdn. zählen
~ **s.b. in** jdn. dazuzählen, beteiligen an

course:
in due ~ zu gegebener Zeit
in the ~ **of time** im Laufe der Zeit
of ~ natürlich

send s.o. to Coventry jdn. gesellschaftlich ächten, schneiden

cover:
~ **a lot of ground** 1. weit herumkommen, 2. umfassend sein

1. We covered a lot of ground during our holiday in France.
2. His talk covered a lot of ground.
~ **for s.o.** jdn. schützen
~ **one's tracks** seine Spuren verwischen
from ~ **to** ~ von Anfang bis Ende (Buch)

crack:
~ **a bottle** eine Flasche köpfen
~ **a joke** einen Witz erzählen
~ **down on s.o.** jdm. gegenüber hart sein
He is ~**ing up.** (Sl.) 1. Er dreht durch., 2. Er lacht sich tot.

cross:
~ a person's path — jdm. in die Quere kommen
~ s.b.'s palm with silver — jdm. Geld geben (für Gefälligkeiten)

He crossed the fortune teller's palm with silver.
~ one's fingers — Daumen drücken

cry:
~ for the moon — das Unmögliche wollen
~ one's heart out — sich die Augen ausweinen
~ing over spilt milk — wegen etwas weinen, das nicht zu ändern ist; sich ärgern

cut:
~ a fine figure — gut aussehen, elegant sein
~ and dried — 1. nicht besonders aufregend, trocken, 2. geplant, vorbereitet

1. His speech was very cut and dried, there was nothing new in it.
2. His plans for leaving were all cut and dried.

~ and thrust — schneller Austausch von Argumenten

A lawyer needs to be quick-witted to survive the cut and thrust of the courtroom.

~ back on s.th. — einschränken, sparen

When the economy is weak the government must cut back on its spending.

~ in on s.o., s.th. — jdn. unterbrechen
~ s.o. dead — jdn. links liegen lassen, schneiden
be ~ out for s.th. — das Zeug zu etwas haben, für etwas wie geschaffen sein

~ s.o., s.th. off short — unterbrechen
~ s.o. to the quick — jdn. zutiefst verletzen
~ no ice (Sl.) — keine Wirkung haben, keinen Einfluss haben

It ~s both ways. — Es hat seine Vor- und Nachteile.
a ~ above s.o.
a short ~ — eine Abkürzung

It is 3 miles to school by road, but there is a short cut through the park.

D

dagger:
look ~s at s.o. (Sl.) — jdn. mit Blicken töten
at ~s drawn — in einem Zustand der offenen Feindschaft, auf Kriegsfuß stehen

dance:
~ attendance — jdm. den Hof machen
~ to s.b.'s tune — nach der Pfeife von jdm. tanzen

dark:
in the ~ — im Ungewissen
I am completely in the dark concerning his plans.
a leap in the ~ — ein Sprung ins kalte Wasser
keep s.th. ~ — etwas geheim halten

dash:
~ s.o.'s hopes — Hoffnungen enttäuschen, zerschlagen
Failing the exam dashed all his hopes of getting a good job.
~ it all! (Sl.) — Verflucht! Verflixt!
~ to pieces — in Stücke schlagen
~ s.th. off — schnell schreiben, erledigen
I'm in a hurry but must just dash off a quick note to my parents.

date:
be up to ~ — modern sein, auf dem neuesten Stand sein
out of ~ — veraltet, unmodern
~ back to — 1. auf eine Zeit zurückgehen, 2. herrühren

1. This cupboard dates back to the 17th century.
2. His limp dates back to his accident.

day:
every other ~ — jeden zweiten Tag
fall on evil ~s — eine Pechsträhne, Unglück haben
have a ~ off — einen freien Tag haben
Let's call it a ~! — Schluss für heute! Feierabend!
one of these ~s — bald, in den nächsten Tagen
see better ~s — bessere Zeiten gesehen haben (fast immer in der Vergangenheit)

The motorcycle had obviously seen better days.
This is not my ~. — Das ist heute nicht mein Tag.
the other ~ — neulich, vor kurzem
this ~ week — heute in einer Woche
this ~ last week — heute vor einer Woche
~ after ~ — täglich, Tag für Tag
~ in and ~ out — den lieben langen Tag, dauernd

dead:
a ~ loss — ein hoffnungsloser Fall
~ and gone — seit langem tot
as ~ as a doornail (engl.) — mausetot
in the ~ of the night — mitten in der Nacht
~ and buried — (bei einer Sache) aus und vorbei, (bei einem Menschen) tot und begraben

That kind of idea is dead and buried.
~ on one's feet — erschöpft
~ tired/beat — todmüde
be ~ to the world — tief und fest schlafen
You must give him a shake to wake him, he's dead to the world.
over my ~ body — nur über meine Leiche
If that dog comes into the house again, it will be over my dead body.

deaf:
turn a ~ ear to s.th. sich einer Sache gegenüber taub stellen

My mother turned a deaf ear to my pleas for a new dress.
be ~ as a post stocktaub sein

deal:
It's a ~! (am./Sl.) Abgemacht!
a great ~ of eine ganze Menge von
~ with sich befassen mit, etwas erledigen
The Managing Director always deals with his post himself.

death:
at ~'s door den Tod vor Augen
The priest was called in as the patient was obviously at death's door.

bore s.o. to ~ jdn. tödlich langweilen
decide in favour of s.o./s.th. sich für jdn./eine Sache entscheiden

be in deep waters das Wasser steht jdm. bis zum Hals

get out of one's depth unsicher werden, ins Schwimmen kommen

The student was out of his depth in discussions on the Middle Ages.

die:
~ a natural death

Never say ~!
~ off

The trees in the wood are dying off.
~ **away**
The wind is gradually dying away.

dig:
~ in

1. natürlich sterben, 2. verschwinden, abklingen
Nur nicht verzweifeln!
dahinsterben, verschwinden, nachlassen

sich legen/beruhigen

1. (sich) eingraben, 2. sich einstellen auf (Sl.), 3. essen, 4. eine Sache anpacken

1. *The wind was so cold the hikers had to dig in for the night half way up the mountain.*
2. *We have a lot of points to discuss, better dig in for a long meeting.*
3. *The hungry man helped himself to a plate of food and dug in.*
4. *If you're worried about the project's outcome just go ahead and dig in!*

~ **s.o./s.th.** (am./Sl.)
I don't dig that kind of thing at all.
~ **s.th. up**
Now where did you dig up that piece of gossip?
Your boyfriend is very good-looking. Where did you dig him up?

jdn./eine Sache verstehen, mögen

herauskramen, aufstöbern, finden

dirt:
throw ~ at s.b.
The election campaign was unfair. A lot of dirt was thrown at the candidate.

jdn. mit Schmutz bewerfen

keep s.b. at a distance
A pretty woman will always have difficulty keeping men at a distance.

jdn. auf Distanz halten

do:
~ **a flip-flop on s.th.** (am.)
The opposition accused the minister of doing a flip-flop too often.

die Meinung ändern

~ away with | beseitigen, töten, aus dem Weg räumen

The murderer didn't know how to do away with the body.

~ s.th. up | etwas renovieren, in Ordnung bringen

~ well with s.b. | gut mit jdm. auskommen

Other people often don't like the boss but I do quite well with him.

nothing ~ing | nichts zu machen

That will ~. | Das geht. Das genügt.

That will do, John. You've had enough ice-cream for today.

~ one's (level) best | sein Bestes geben

~ one's bit (Sl.) | seinen Teil erledigen, seine Pflicht tun

~ s.th. the hard way | etwas ungeschickt anstellen

Don't try to hit that nail in with your shoe, that's doing it the hard way.

~ s.th. up | etwas reparieren

Don't let s.o./s.th. get you down. | Lass dich von niemandem/nichts kleinkriegen.

Don't look a gift horse in the mouth. (Sprichw.) | Einem geschenkten Gaul schaut man nicht ins Maul.

dog:
Every ~ has its day. | Jeder hat irgendwann einmal Glück.
Lead a ~'s life | ein Hundeleben führen
go to the ~s (Sl.) | vor die Hunde gehen
Let sleeping ~s lie. | Schlafende Hunde soll man nicht wecken.

doubt:

beyond a ~/without a ~ | zweifellos

Without a doubt, that's the best cake I have ever tasted.

in ~ | unsicher

If in doubt, follow your instincts.

shadow of a ~ | leichte Ungewissheit

down:
~ at (the) heel(s) | schäbig, heruntergekommen
go ~ the drain | in die Binsen gehen, für die Katz' sein

~ to earth   ehrlich, offen, vernünftig
have a ~ on s.b.   jdn. auf dem Kieker haben
He's had a down on me ever since I won the prize.

drag:
~ one's feet   sich dahinschleppen, langsam machen

If you drag your feet you'll not get the contract.
~ s.th. out   in die Länge ziehen
~ on   (sich) in die Länge ziehen
The talk was boring and dragged on for hours.

draw:
~ in one's horns (Sl.)   sich krumm legen müssen, sparen
~ a blank   eine Niete ziehen, nicht weiterkommen
~ one's last breath   seinen letzten Atemzug tun
~ s.b.'s attention to   jds. Aufmerksamkeit lenken auf
~ the line at   die Grenze ziehen bei
~ s.th. to a close   etwas zu Ende bringen, abschließen

The days are ~ing in.   Die Tage werden kürzer.

dressed to kill (Sl.)   sehr fein angezogen, aufgetakelt wie eine Fregatte, herausgeputzt

drive:
~ a hard bargain   harte Bedingungen stellen
~ a wedge between   einen Keil treiben zwischen
~ into a corner   in die Ecke treiben
~ to despair   zur Verzweiflung bringen
~ s.o. nuts (am./Sl.)   jdn. wahnsinnig machen
The sound of his voice is driving me nuts.
~ s.o. crazy/mad/potty (engl./Sl.)   jdn. auf die Palme bringen
~ at s.th.   auf etwas hinauswollen
You know what I'm driving at.   Du weißt, worauf ich hinaus will.
~ s.th. home to s.o.   jdm. etwas klar machen
~ s.o. up the wall (Sl.)   jdn. verrückt machen
One day, all my troubles will drive me up the wall.

drop:
~ **by** ~	tropfenweise
~ **by**	vorbeischauen
~ **in**	unerwartet vorbeikommen
~ **it!** (Sl.)	Lass das!
a ~ **in the ocean**	ein Tropfen auf dem heißen Stein
~ **a brick** (Sl.)	ins Fettnäpfchen treten
~ **dead!** (Sl.)	Scher dich zum Teufel!
~ **off (to sleep)**	einnicken, einschlafen
~ **s.o. a line**	jdm. ein paar Zeilen schreiben

drum s.th. into s.b. jdm. etwas einhämmern

like a dying duck in a thunderstorm (engl./Sl.) wie der Ochse vor dem Berg, keine Ahnung haben

due:
give the devil his ~ dem Kaiser geben, was des Kaisers ist
in ~ time zur rechten Zeit

stand there like a stuffed dummy (Sl.) wie Ölgötzen dastehen

dust:
bite the ~ (Sl.) ins Gras beißen
throw ~ in s.o.'s eyes jdm. Sand in die Augen streuen

Dutch courage (Sl.) angetrunkener Mut
He had a couple of drinks at the bar to give him Dutch courage to face his wife.

E

ear:
be all ~s — ganz Ohr sein
be up to one's ~s in work — bis über beide Ohren in Arbeit stecken

fall on deaf ~s — tauben Ohren predigen
give one's ~s for s.th. — alles für etwas geben
(play) by ~ — 1. nach Gehör spielen, 2. improvisieren

1. She plays the piano entirely by ear.
2. I haven't decided yet what to tell him, I'll play it by ear.
turn a deaf ~ — nicht auf etwas hören
He turned a deaf ear to all advice.
keep an ~ to the ground — Augen und Ohren offen halten
pin back s.o.'s ~s — jdn. übers Ohr hauen

ease:
at ~ — zwanglos, bequem
~ off s.th. — 1. sich befreien von, 2. erleichtern
He eased off his shoes gently as his feet were sore.
They eased off his task.
feel ill at ~ — sich unbehaglich/nicht wohl in seiner Haut fühlen

easy:
~ does it! (Sl.) — Lass dir Zeit, Vorsicht!
~ on the eye — gefällig, schön anzusehen
on ~ terms — zu günstigen Bedingungen
Take it ~! — Immer mit der Ruhe!
in ~ circumstances — finanziell gesichert

eat:
~ away — 1. nagen (an), langsam entfernen, 2. ärgern, Sorge machen

1. The sea has eaten away much of the shore.
2. Fear of not passing the exam was eating away at her.
~ humble pie (Sl.) — sich demütigen

~ **like a bird/sparrow** (Sl.)	nur kleine Portionen essen, essen wie ein Spatz
~ **one's words**	seine Worte zurücknehmen
~ **out**	essen gehen
~ **like a horse** (Sl.)	essen wie ein Scheunendrescher

~ **s.b. out of house and home**	jdm. die Haare vom Kopf fressen
~ **one's head off**	viel essen
~ **one's heart out**	sehr traurig sein

John ate his heart out when he had to leave home.

egg:
as sure as ~**s is** ~**s** (Sl.)	so sicher wie das Amen in der Kirche; man kann sich drauf verlassen
~ **s.o. on**	jdn. ermutigen

The boy only threw the stone because the others egged him on.

have one over eight (Sl.)	einen über den Durst trinken

elbow:
~ **one's way**	sich hindurchdrängen, sich durchboxen
have at one's ~	bei der Hand haben
at the eleventh hour	in letzter Minute, fünf vor zwölf, kurz bevor es zu spät ist

end:
come to an ~	enden
My hair stands on ~.	Die Haare stehen mir zu Berge.
put an ~ to s.th.	einer Sache ein Ende bereiten/machen
~ up	enden
You'll end up in jail.	
All's well that ~s well.	Ende gut, alles gut.
to no ~	zwecklos

engage:
~ in politics	sich in der Politik engagieren
~ in small talk	Belangloses reden

enough:
~ is as good as a feast. (Sprichw.)	Allzuviel ist ungesund.
~ and to spare	reichlich, mehr als genug
~ to go round	genug für alle, reichlich

enter:
~ one's mind/head	in den Sinn kommen
~ into s.th.	etwas anfangen, sich auf etwas einlassen

get even with s.o.   es jdm. heimzahlen

every:
~ cloud has a silver lining. (Sprichw.)	In allem Schlechten liegt das Gute im Ansatz verborgen. Wo Schatten ist, ist auch Licht.
~ now and then	hin und wieder, dann und wann
~ other day	jeden zweiten Tag

everything:
~ but the kitchen sink (engl./Sl.)	absolut alles
~ from soup to nuts (am./Sl.)	absolut alles

eye:
make s.b. open his ~s	jdm. die Augen öffnen
never take one's ~s off s.th.	die Augen nicht abwenden
with an ~ to	mit Rücksicht auf
see ~ to ~	übereinstimmen

raise one's eyebrows   die Stirne runzeln

F

face:
~ to ~ — von Angesicht zu Angesicht, Auge in Auge
~ the music (Sl.) — Zorn über sich ergehen lassen
The boy broke the window and had to face the music when his father came home.
be ~d with — mit etwas konfrontiert werden/sein
~ up to a failure — einer Niederlage ins Gesicht sehen
have the ~ to do s.th. — die Stirn haben, etwas zu tun
on the ~ of it — auf den ersten Blick, anscheinend
pull a ~ at s.o. — Grimassen schneiden
show one's ~ — sich sehen lassen
I hate family gatherings, but I must at least show my face.
take s.th. at ~ value — etwas für bare Münze nehmen
keep a straight ~ — ernst bleiben, nicht lachen
It was very difficult to keep a straight face as the clown performed his tricks.

fact:
as a matter of ~ — in der Tat, tatsächlich
know s.th. for a ~ — etwas genau wissen

fall:
~ all over s.o. (Sl.) — um jdm. viel Aufhebens machen
My friend falls all over my daughter, whenever she comes to visit.
~ back on s.o./s.th. — jdn. um Hilfe bitten, auf etwas zurückgreifen
~ down on the job — etwas nicht richtig machen, mit einer Arbeit nicht zurechtkommen
~ flat on one's face (Sl.) — auf die Nase fallen, ohne Erfolg sein
~ for s.o. (Sl.) — sich verlieben
~ on deaf ears — auf taube Ohren stoßen
~ on one's feet — wie eine Katze immer wieder auf die Füße fallen
~ over backwards to do s.th. — sich beinahe überschlagen, etwas zu tun

~ in place   in Ordnung kommen, klar werden
*When he told me his story, all the facts
I had known before fell into place.*
~ out with s.o.   sich mit jdn. zanken/überwerfen
~ through   nichts werden

far:
~-fetched   an den Haaren herbeigezogen, weit hergeholt
~ from it!   überhaupt nicht!

favour:
in ~ of   zugunsten von
Would you do me a ~?   Können Sie mir einen Gefallen tun?

feather:
a ~ in one's cap   eine Ehre, eine Belohnung
*John earned a feather in his cap
by winning the race.*

~ one's nest   seine Schäfchen ins Trockene bringen

to be fed up with s.o./s.th. (Sl.)   etwas/jdn. dick haben, genug von etwas/jdm. haben

feel:
~ free to do s.th.   das Gefühl haben, etwas tun zu dürfen

~ **out of place** — sich nicht wie zu Hause, sich fehl am Platz fühlen

~ **like doing s.th.** — Lust haben, etwas zu tun
~ **for s.o.** — es jdm. nachfühlen können
~ **s.th. in one's bones** — etwas im Gefühl haben

fiddle:
play second ~ — nicht die erste Geige spielen
~ **around with s.th.** — an etwas herumspielen

figure out (am./Sl.) — schätzen, erraten

find one's feet — zurechtkommen
After a year in the job I'm beginning to find my feet.

finger:
have a ~ **in the pie** (Sl.) — die Hand im Spiel haben
His ~**s are all thumbs.** — Er hat zwei linke Hände.
He won't raise a ~. — Er macht keinen Finger krumm.
twist s.b. round one's little ~ — jdn. um den kleinen Finger wickeln

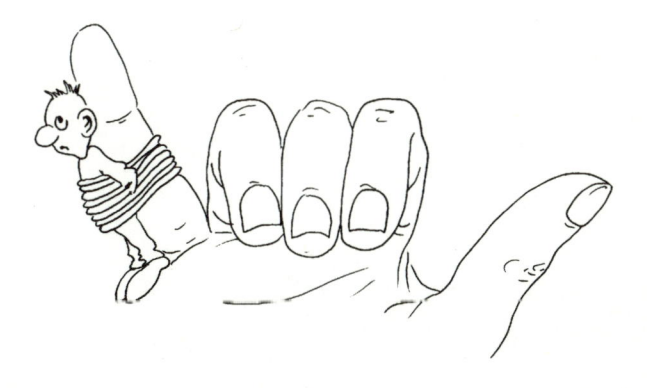

first:
~ **and foremost** — zunächst einmal, vor allem anderen
at ~ **sight** — auf den ersten Blick
~ **come** ~ **served.** — Wer zuerst kommt, mahlt zuerst.
from ~ **to last** — die ganze Zeit

fish:
have other ~ **to fry** — Wichtigeres zu tun haben
That's a bit ~**y!** — Das ist nicht ganz geheuer/legal.

fit:
give s.b. a ~ — jdm. einen Schock versetzen
be ~ as a fiddle — gesund wie ein Fisch im Wasser sein

It's not ~ for her. — Es schickt sich nicht für sie.

flat:
to be singing ~ — falsch singen
~ out (Sl.) — klar und deutlich
They told me flat out that they were reporting me to the police.

flesh:
neither ~, fowl nor good red herring — weder Fisch noch Fleisch
put on ~ — dick werden
make s.o.'s ~ creep — jdm. einen Schrecken einjagen
~ s.th. out — anschaulich machen

have a fling (Sl.) — das Leben genießen (sich gehen lassen)

fly:
~ into a rage — in Wut geraten
~-by-night — unzuverlässig(er) Mensch
~ off the handle — die Beherrschung verlieren, aus der Haut fahren

follow:
~ **in s.b.'s footsteps**	in jds. Fußstapfen treten
~ **one's nose** (Sl.)	geradeaus gehen, immer der Nase nach
~ **one's suit**	es jdm. gleich tun

fool:
live in a ~'s paradise	in trügerischer Sicherheit leben
make a ~ of o.s.	sich zum Narren machen

foot:
be (back) on one's feet	(wieder) auf den Beinen sein
have one ~ in the grave	mit einem Fuß im Grab stehen
~ **the bill**	die Rechnung bezahlen
have feet of clay	eine verborgene Schwäche haben, auch nur ein Mensch sein

He may be a dictator, but his feet are of clay.

put one's ~ down	entschlossen handeln, einschreiten

for:
~ **one**	zum Beispiel
~ **all I care**	Es ist mir egal.
~ **all I know**	so viel ich weiß
~ **chicken feed** (am./Sl.)	für fast gar nichts, für ein paar Pfennige, für 'nen Appel und ein Ei
~ **good**	für immer
~ **hours on end**	stundenlang
~ **sure**	gewiss
~ **the fun of it** (Sl.)	nur aus Spaß
~ **the time being**	zunächst

forever and a day	für immer und ewig

Fortune favours fools. (Sl.)	Mancher hat mehr Glück als Verstand.

free:
make ~ with s.th.	mit etwas umgehen, als gehöre es einem
make ~ with s.b.	sich jdm. gegenüber viel herausnehmen
~ **and easily**	lässig
~**-handed**	großzügig

45

from:
- **pillar to post** — von Ort zu Ort
- **bad to worse** — vom Regen in die Traufe
- **rags to riches** — von Armut zum Reichtum
- **the outset** — von Anfang an
- **top to bottom** — durch die Bank

front:
have the ~ to do s.th. — die Stirn haben, etwas zu tun
put on a bold ~ — einer Sache tapfer ins Gesicht sehen; tun, als ob man keine Angst hat

When you are afraid of a dog, it's best to just put on a bold front.

full:
~ of hot air — voller Unsinn, unnützes Zeug (reden)
~ of beans — glücklich, übermütig
at ~ length — in voller Länge
~ well — sehr wohl (adv.)
He knew full well that he was wrong.

fuss:
make no ~ about s.th. — nicht viel Aufhebens machen
~ about — Aufhebens machen um

G

gain on s.b./s.th. — sich jdm./etwas nähern, aufholen
In the race, the American athlete kept gaining on his English rival.

game:
make ~ of s.b. — auf Kosten von jdm. Spaß haben, jdn. zum Besten halten
The ~'s up. — Das Spiel ist aus.
have the ~ in one's hands — die Sache fest im Griff haben
play the ~ — sich an die Spielregeln halten
Cheating is not fair. You must learn to play the game.

gas up (am./Sl.) — (auf)tanken

run the gauntlet — Spießruten laufen

get:
~ **above o.s.** — sich überschätzen
~ **ahead** — vorankommen, Karriere machen
~ **along with s.o.** — mit jdm. auskommen
They got along well from the moment they met.
~ **along without s.o.** — ohne etwas auskommen
~ **away** — 1. entwischen, entkommen, 2. wegkommen, in Urlaub gehen

1. *The police gave chase but the thief got away.*
2. *I have worked so hard lately, I must get away for a few days.*

~ **behind with** — in Rückstand geraten mit
I can't take time off to go to the cinema. I'm getting behind with my work.
~ **carried away** — sich mitreißen lassen
~ **down to business** — zur Sache kommen
~ **in touch with** — Kontakt aufnehmen mit, anrufen
~ **it over and done with** — etwas ein und für alle Mal hinter sich bringen
~ **one's teeth into s.th.** — sich in etwas verbeißen
~ **out of hand** — außer Kontrolle geraten
We must discuss the situation carefully, before it gets out of hand.
~ **rid of s.th.** — etwas loswerden
~ **s.th. off one's chest** — sich etwas von der Seele reden
Once she had got the whole story off her chest she felt better.
~ **to grips with s.b.** — sich mit jdm. auseinandersetzen
~ **to the bottom of s.th.** — einer Sache auf den Grund gehen
The police haver never really got to the bottom of that crime.
It ~s about. — Es spricht sich herum.
~ **a break** — Glück haben
The applicant hoped he would get a break and win the competition.
~ **a hand** — Applaus bekommen
The singer got a good hand at the end of the concert.

~ **a move on** (Sl.)	von etwas angemacht werden
~ **a load off one's mind** (Sl.)	etwas loswerden
~ **cracking** (Sl.)	etwas Dampf machen, loslegen

We'll never finish the job in time if we don't get cracking.

~ **down to brass tacks** (Sl.)	Tacheles reden
~ **down to the nitty-gritty**	zur Sache kommen
~ **goose bumps** (am.)/ **goose pimples** (engl.)	eine Gänsehaut bekommen
~ **mad at s.o.**	sich über jdn. ärgern

I got so mad with my daughter, I wanted to slap her.

~ **on s.o.'s nerves**	jdm. auf die Nerven gehen
~ **one's act together** (Sl.)	Ordnung in die Sache bringen, sich am Riemen reißen

I must get act together, before I present my project to the committee.

~ **one's fingers burned**	sich die Finger verbrennen (auch wörtlich)
~ **out of the wrong side of bed**	mit dem falschen Fuß aufstehen
~ **s.th. under one's belt** (Sl.)	sich etwas 'reinziehen

I'm so hungry, I'd feel much better if I got a good meal under my belt.

~ **the boot**	den Laufpass kriegen
~ **the sack** (Sl.)	entlassen werden
~**-up-and-go**	Energie, Tatkraft, Motivation

Just look at John, he can't wait to start the game. He's full of get-up-and-go.

give:

~ **as good as one gets**	es jdm. mit gleicher Münze heimzahlen

Peter can take care of himself in an argument. He can give as good as he gets.

~ **birth to**	zur Welt bringen
~ **cause for**	Grund geben für
~ **chase**	verfolgen
~ **credit where credit is due**	Ehre wem Ehre gebührt, Anerkennung zollen

Let's give credit where credit is due, you have written a marvellous book.

~ **ear to**	anhören
~ **s.o. free rein**	jdm. freie Hand lassen

We gave the au-pair girl free rein with the care of the children.

~ **of one's best**	sein Bestes geben
~ **o.s. airs**	sich aufspielen

Don't be so superior, stop giving yourself airs!

~ **out**	kaputtgehen

My washing-machine has finally given out on me, I must buy a new one.

~ **rise to s.th.**	etwas verursachen

The bad state of the building gave rise to much criticism.

~ **s.o. a dirty look**	jdn. böse anschauen

He gave his father a dirty look when he criticised him.

~ **s.o. a hand with s.th.**	jdm. bei etwas helfen

Will you give me a hand to move the furniture for the party?

~ **s.o. away**	verraten, ausplaudern
~ **s.o. trouble**	jdm. Schwierigkeiten machen
~ **s.o. the creeps**	jdn. erschrecken
~ **s.o. the green light**	jdm. grünes Licht geben
~ **the game away** (Sl.)	einen Plan verraten
~ **up the ghost** (Sl.)	sterben
~ **up a secret**	ein Geheimnis preisgeben
~ **way to**	Platz machen

glance:

~ **at**	einen Blick werfen

~ over s.th. etwas überfliegen, den Blick schweifen lassen

He merely glanced over the paper, he didn't have time to read it carefully.

catch a glimpse of nur flüchtig zu sehen bekommen

be hand in glove with s.o. mit jdm. unter einer Decke stecken

go:
a ~ ein Versuch
have a ~ (Sl.) 1. versuchen, 2. an die Reihe kommen

1. You can do it if you try, have a go.
2. It's my go to throw the ball.

~ about one's business sich um seine eigenen Angelegenheiten kümmern

~ about s.th. herangehen an, in Angriff nehmen
~ against the grain gegen den Strich gehen

It goes very much against the grain to admit that my enemy is right.

~ ahead mach weiter, nur zu
~ at each other aufeinander losgehen, streiten
~ back on one's word ein Versprechen/Wort nicht halten
~ bananas (am./Sl.) verrückt werden
~ behind s.o.'s back jdn. hintergehen
~ beyond one's duty seine Kompetenz überschreiten
~ by s.o.'s opinion sich nach jds. Meinung richten
~ by the board verloren gehen; kaputt gehen

Your plan has gone by the board, the trip has been cancelled.

~ by the rules sich an die Regeln halten
~ cold turkey (am./Sl.) sofort aufhören, etwas abbrechen

When drug addicts go cold turkey they become very ill.

~ down fighting bis zum bitteren Ende kämpfen
~ down in history in die Geschichte eingehen

The last decade was a time of such tremendous change. I'm sure it will go down in history.

~ downhill sich rapide verschlechtern

He has gone downhill since his wife left him.

~ down the drain schief gehen

~ **Dutch**	die Kosten teilen
~ **easy on s.o.**	lieb/vorsichtig mit jdm. sein
~ **from bad to worse**	immer schlechter werden
~ **off the deep end**	überstürzt, den Gefühlen gehorchend, handeln

He has gone completely off the deep end with his new girl-friend.

~ **one better**	es besser machen
~ **places** (Sl.)	eine Zukunft haben

Cecilia is a very talented actess, she will obviously go places.

~ **round the bend**	1. um die Kurve fahren, 2. verrückt werden
~ **sky high** (Sl.)	ins Unermessliche steigen, sehr hoch hinaufgehen

Prices have gone sky high.

~ **straight** (Sl.)	ein neues, ehrliches Leben beginnen
~ **through the roof**	vor Wut an die Decke gehen

John got so angry with his dog he almost went through the roof.

~ **to pieces**	1. kaputtgehen, zu Bruch gehen, 2. zusammenbrechen

1. *My ball-dress is so old it is going to pieces.*
2. *When she heard of his death she went to pieces.*

~ to town (Sl.) 1. hart/schnell arbeiten, 2. übertrieben viel Geld ausgeben

1. Just look how fast they are working, they really are going to town.
2. The really went to town about entertaining their friends.

That just goes to show that... Das beweist nur, dass ...
That goes without saying. Das versteht sich von selbst.

good:
as ~ as it gets besser wird's nicht
I know everything is far from perfect, but I'm afraid this is as good as it gets.
It's no ~ crying. Es nützt nichts, wenn du weinst.
~ for nothing zu nichts nütze, Tunichtgut, Taugenichts

~ gracious! Du meine Güte!
for ~ für immer

goose:
He wouldn't say "boo" to a ~. (Sl.) Er hat/zeigt nie Mut.

It's all Greek to me. Für mich sind das böhmische Dörfer.

go green with envy (Sl.) vor Neid platzen

grin and bear it (Sl.) in den sauren Apfel beißen

grit one's teeth die Zähne zusammenbeißen
The only way to face something unpleasant is to grit one's teeth and bear it.

ground:
be dashed to the ~ am Boden zerstört sein
be well ~ed in bewandert sein in
There's no doubt he'll pass the examination, he's so well-groundet in all the subjects.
stay one's ~ sich behaupten

grow:
~ in strength stärker (zahlreicher) werden

~ out of s.th. | 1. aus etwas herauswachsen, 2. zu alt für etwas werden

1. *John has grown out of his shoes yet again.*
2. *I'm twenty now and have grown out of such childish things.*

~ up | 1. heranwachsen, 2. körperlich und geistig reif werden

Oh, for goodness' sake grow up and act your age!

gun:
~ for s.o. (Sl.) | jdn. suchen, um ihm zu schaden, strafen

The headmaster is gunning for you, he knows you missed the cricket match.

a big ~ (Sl.) | ein wichtiger, einflussreicher Mensch

stick to one's ~s | seinen Standpunkt fest behaupten

H

habit:
break a ~ | sich etwas abgewöhnen
make a ~ of s.th. | sich etwas zur Gewohnheit machen

hail:
within ~ | in Rufweite
~ from | ursprünglich herstammen/kommen

hair:
keep one's ~ on | sich beherrschen
a ~ of the dog that bit you (Sl.) | ein Schluck Alkohol gegen den Kater

split ~s | über unwichtige, banale Sachen streiten, Haarspaltereien betreiben

My ~'s standing on end. | Die Haare stehen mir zu Berge.
I was so afraid my hair stood on end.
hale and hearty | gesund

half:
~-baked — noch grün hinter den Ohren
~ seas over (engl./Sl.) — betrunken
~ a loaf is better than no bread. (Sprichw.) — Der Spatz in der Hand ist besser als die Taube auf dem Dach.

hammer:
~ at s.th. — eifrig an etwas arbeiten
~ s.th. into s.b. — jdm. etwas einbläuen
It took the teacher all morning to hammer the theory into his pupils.
~ and tongs — mit viel Lärm/Kraft/Enthusiasmus
He may not be any good as a pianist but he certainly goes at it hammer and tongs.
~ out (engl./Sl.) — nach vielen Diskussionen zu einer Entscheidung kommen

We spent all weekend hammering out our plans for the future.

hand:
an old ~ — ein Mensch mit viel Erfahrung
Let me help. I'm an old hand at mending things.
at first ~ — aus erster Hand
change ~s — den Besitzer wechseln
This house has changed hands many times.
do s.th. off ~ — etwas aus dem Stegreif tun, etwas nebenbei tun
~ down to — vererben, weitergeben an
on the other ~ — andererseits
~ in glove with s.o. — sehr eng, nahe
The doctor and his nursing staff really work hand in glove.
out of ~ — außer Kontrolle
~-me-down — ein weitergereichtes Kleidungsstück
Why can't I have a new dress? I hate always wearing hand-me-downs.
~ over fist — sehr schnell

have a ~ in s.th. — teilhaben an, die Finger in einer Angelegenheit haben

handle:
~ **with kid gloves** — vorsichtig umgehen mit, mit Samthandschuhen behandeln

hang:
~ **back** — zögern, sich sträuben
~ **by a single thread** — am seidenen Faden hängen
~ **in the balance** — unentschlossen sein
~ **one's head** — den Kopf hängen lassen
~ **on** — 1. warten, durchhalten 2. (Sl.) Ausdauer zeigen

1. Hang on, I'm just ready.
2. The plan hasn't worked yet but I mean to hang on until it does.

~ **on s.b.'s lips/words** — an jds. Lippen hängen
~ **out** (Sl.) — hausen, sich aufhalten, verkehren mit

I'm afraid Mary might be hanging out with the wrong people.

~ **together** — logisch sein, schlüssig sein

Your story doesn't hang together. You must be making it up.

~ **up** — den Telefonhörer auflegen/aufhängen

happen:
~ **on s.b.** — zufällig auf jdn. treffen

I walked into the library and happened on John and David.

~ **what may** (engl.) — Was auch immer geschieht!

hard:
be ~ **on s.b.** — jdm. schwer zusetzen
~ **and fast** — strikt, straff, dauerhaft

In view of her illness, we cannot make any hard and fast arrangements.

a ~ **nut to crack** — ein schwieriger Mensch, eine schwierige Situation

~ **on s.o.'s heels** — dicht hinterher
~ **put to do s.th.** — etwas mit Schwierigkeiten tun
~ **up** (Sl.) — blank, ohne Kohle

hare:
~**-brained** — dumm, unverantwortlich

run with the ~ and hunt with the hounds (Sl.)	auf zwei Hochzeiten tanzen
be out of harm's way	außer Gefahr sein, keinen Unfug anrichten können
make a hash of s.th.	Chaos anrichten, etwas in den Sand setzen
eat one's hat	einen Besen fressen

bury the hatchet	das Kriegsbeil begraben
have:	
~ a bone to pick with s.b.	mit jdm. ein Hühnchen zu rupfen haben
~ a close shave	glimpflich davonkommen
~ a fit (Sl.)	einen Wutanfall bekommen
~ a fling with s.o.	mit jdm. eine Affäre haben
~ a go at s.th.	etwas versuchen
~ a good command of s.th.	etwas beherrschen/gut können
He has a good command of English.	
~ a good head on one's shoulders	intelligent sein, ein kluger Kopf sein
~ a hand in s.th.	die Hand im Spiel haben
~ a hold over s.b.	jdn. in der Hand haben
~ a mind to	Lust haben zu
~ a near miss	knapp (mit dem Leben) davonkommen

~ **a screw loose** (Sl.)	eine Schraube locker haben
~ **a sweet tooth**	gern Süßes essen

Jane loves ice-cream.
She has a sweet tooth.

~ **a swelled head** (am./Sl.)	eingebildet sein
~ **a whale of a time** (Sl.)	sehr viel Spaß haben
~ **a word with s.o.**	mit jdm. ein Wörtchen reden
~ **ants in one's pants**	unruhig sein, rastlos sein
~ **had one's fill**	gesättigt sein
~ **one's feet on the ground**	mit beiden Beinen auf dem Boden stehen
~ **one's finger in the pie**	bei einer Sache mitmachen
~ **one's head in the clouds**	geistesabwesend sein
~ **one's heart in one's mouth**	sein Herz auf der Zunge tragen
~ **one's way**	es machen, wie man will; sich durchsetzen
~ **one's wits about one**	alle seine Sinne beieinander haben
~ **a row with s.o.**	Streit mit jdm. haben
~ **second thoughts**	Zweifel bekommen
~ **s.th. up one's sleeve**	ein Geheimnis/eine Überraschung parat haben
~ **s.th. wrapped up**	etwas erklärt/erledigt haben
~ **the courage of one's convictions**	Zivilcourage haben
~ **the gift of the gab** (Sl.)	gut im Reden sein, überzeugend
~ **the guts to do s.th.** (Sl.)	den Mumm haben, etwas zu tun
~ **too many irons in the fire**	zu viel auf einmal anpacken, sich verzetteln
~ **what it takes**	das gewisse Etwas haben
Make hay while the sun shines.	das Eisen schmieden, solange es heiß ist

head:

not make ~ or tail of s.th.	sich keinen Reim auf etwas machen können, aus etwas nicht klug werden
have a good ~ on one's shoulders	ein kluger Kopf sein
keep one's ~	einen kühlen Kopf behalten
keep one's ~ above water	sich über Wasser halten können
be ~ over heels in love	bis über beide Ohren verliebt sein
talk one's ~ off	sich dumm und dusselig reden
take the ~	die Führung übernehmen
run ~ over heels	Hals über Kopf davonstürzen
~ and shoulders above	weit voraus/überlegen

have one's ~ screwed on the right way   intelligent/klug sein
John will make the right decision. He has his head screwed on the right way.
~ on   frontal

hear:
~ s.o. out   jdn. ausreden lassen
in my ~ing   in meiner Gegenwart
~ from s.o.   eine Botschaft/einen Brief von jdm. bekommen

heart:
after one's own ~   nach dem eigenem Geschmack
break s.o.'s ~   jdm. das Herz brechen
find it in one's ~ to   es übers Herz bringen
I could not find it in my heart to tell him.
have one's ~ in one's boots (Sl.)   sehr deprimiert sein, Angst haben
learn s.th. by ~   etwas auswendig lernen
lose ~   den Mut verlieren
lose one's ~ to s.o.   sein Herz an jdn. verlieren
take s.th. to ~   sich etwas zu Herzen nehmen
wear one's ~ on one's sleeves   aus seinem Herzen keine Mördergrube machen, ganz offen sein

heel:
take on one's ~s   die Beine in die Hand nehmen, ausreißen

When I saw the bull in the field, I took to my heels and fled.
kick one's ~s   Zeit verschwenden/vertrödeln

help:
~ o.s. to s.th.   sich etwas nehmen, sich bedienen
~ s.b. with s.th.   jdm. etwas behilflich sein

high:
~ and dry   verlassen
~ and mighty   arrogant
~-flyer   ein ehrgeiziger Mensch, der es zu etwas bringt
~-handed   arrogant
fly ~   ehrgeizig sein

hint:
drop a ~ einen dezenten Hinweis geben
give a broad ~ einen Wink mit dem Zaunpfahl geben

take a ~ einen Wink verstehen

hit:
~ at s.th. nach etwas schlagen
~ bottom (Sl.) einen Tiefpunkt erreichen
~ on stoßen auf
~ or miss auf gut Glück
~ s.o. below the belt jdn. unter der Gürtellinie treffen
~ the ceiling (Sl.) in die Luft gehen (vor Wut)
~ the sack (Sl.) ins Bett gehen, sich aufs Ohr hauen

~ the nail on the head den Nagel auf den Kopf treffen

hold:
have a ~ of s.th. etwas beherrschen
~ in high regard hoch achten, in Ehren halten
~ all the aces (Sl.) alle Asse in der Hand halten, eine gute Ausgangsposition haben

Don't ~ your breath. Warte gar nicht erst darauf, dass es passiert!

~ forth lang reden, sich auslassen
Janet is incredibly boring. She can hold forth for ages on the most uninteresting subjects.

~ **one's own**   sich behaupten
A shy person always has difficulty holding his own in an argument.
~ **one's peace**   sich nicht einmischen, still/ruhig bleiben
~ **one's tongue**   nicht sprechen, den Mund halten
~ **the line!**   Bleiben Sie bitte am Apparat!
~ **true**   sich bewahrheiten
take ~ **of s.th.**   Besitz ergreifen von

home:
drive s.th. ~ **to s.b.**   jdm. etwas klarmachen
It took me a long time to drive the point home to him.
hit ~   ins Schwarze treffen
make o.s. at ~   es sich bequem machen

hook:
on one's own ~   auf eigene Faust
by ~ **or by crook**   auf Biegen und Brechen
off the ~   aus der Klemme
play ~**y** (am./Sl.)   Schule schwänzen

Nobody cares two hoots about it.   Danach kräht kein Hahn.

honour:
a debt of ~   Ehrenschulden
a point of ~   Ehrensache

hop:
keep s.b. on the hop   jdm. in Ruhe lassen
be ~**ping mad** (Sl.)   stinksauer sein
~ **to it!** (Sl.)   Beweg' dich! Mach schnell!

hope:
~ **for the best**   das Beste hoffen
against all ~   gegen jede Vernunft auf etwas zu hoffen

stir up a hornet's nest   in ein Wespennest stechen

horse:
a dark ~   eine unbekannte Größe
a ~ **of a different colour**   eine ganz andere Sache

have ~ sense	einen gesunden Menschenverstand haben
on one's high ~	von oben herab
straight from the ~'s mouth	aus erster Hand
~ play (Sl.)	herumtoben
Reckon without one's host.	Die Rechnung ohne den Wirt machen.

hot:

~ and bothered	aufgeregt, ängstlich

The witness grew hot and bothered when the judge asked him a question.

get into ~ water (Sl.)	in Teufels Küche kommen
go like ~ cakes	weggehen wie warme Semmeln
~ under the collar	wütend, verlegen, durcheinander

house:

bring down the ~	hervorragend spielen (Theater)
keep (an) open ~	Leute zu jeder Zeit willkommen heißen
like a ~ on fire	schnell, mit Elan

She was working away like a house on fire.

how:

~ about ...?	Wie wär's mit ...?
~ are things?	Wie geht's?
hug o.s. about s.th.	sich selbst zu etwas beglückwünschen/gratulieren
eat humble pie	kleinlaut werden

hunt:

~ after s.th.	etwas nachjagen
~ for/up	suchen
~ s.b. down	jdn. zur Strecke bringen

hurry:

be in a ~	in Eile sein, es eilig haben
~ over s.th.	etwas hastig tun/erledigen
~ up!	Beeile dich!

I

keep s.th. on ice — eine Sache auf Eis legen

idea:
form an ~ of s.th. — sich eine Vorstellung von etwas machen

put ~s into s.o.'s head — jdm. Flausen in den Kopf setzen
What's the big ~? — Was soll das? Was hast du für einen Unsinn vor?

If the worst comes to the worst ... — Wenn alle Stricke reißen, ..., Wenn wirklich alles schief läuft, ...

ill:
~ at ease — unwohl (in der Haut), ängstlich, nervös

~-assorted — inkompatibel; schlecht zueinander passend

It's an ~ bird that fouls its own nest. (Sprichw.) — Das eigene Nest beschmutzt man nicht.
~ weeds grow apace. (Sprichw.) — Unkraut vergeht nicht.

impose:
~ on s.b. — jdm. zur Last fallen
~ o.s. on s.b. — sich jdm. aufdrängen

improve on s.th. — etwas besser machen

in:
- **~ a bad way** — in schlechter Verfassung
- **~ a flash** (Sl.) — schnell, sofort
- **~ a fog** — geistesabwesend, unachtsam
- **~ a huff** — eingeschnappt
- **~ a lather** (Sl.) — aufgeregt, durcheinander, erhitzt
- **~ a nutshell** — knapp ausgedrückt, kurz gefasst
- **~ a quandary** — konfus, durcheinander
- **~ a tight spot** — in Schwierigkeiten
- **~ a vicious circle** — in einem Teufelskreis
- **~ appel-pie order** (am./Sl.) — in guter Verfassung, ordentlich
- **~ bad taste** — geschmacklos

To laugh at a funeral is in very bad taste.

~ **broad daylight**	am helllichten Tag
~ **cold blood** (Sl.)	grausam, kaltblütig
~ **deep** (am./Sl.)	in größten Schwierigkeiten, verschuldet
~ **due course**	zur richtigen Zeit, mit der Zeit
~ **fine feather**	gut gelaunt

~ **full swing** voll im Gange
The party was in full swing when I arrived.
~ **for a penny,** ~ **for a pound.** (engl./Sl.) Wer A sagt, muss auch B sagen.
~ **for it** (Sl.) vor Schwierigkeiten stehen
~ **good time** schnell, in kurzer Zeit
~ **hot water** (Sl.) in Schwierigkeiten
~ **less than no time** im Nu
~ **no time (at all)** sehr schnell
~ **one ear and out the other** zum einen Ohr hinein zum anderen hinaus

~ **one's cup** betrunken
He is likely to start a fight when he's in his cups.
~ **one's mind's eye** vor dem inneren Auge
~ **one's Sunday best** im Sonntagskleid/-staat
~ **short supply** rar
~ **the bag** (Sl.) gewiss, sicher
~ **the doghouse** (Sl.) in Schwierigkeiten
~ **the long run** auf lange Sicht, endlich, zum Schluss

~ **the middle of nowhere**	dort, wo sich Fuchs und Hase „Gute Nacht" sagen
~ **the prime of life**	im besten Alter
~ **the twinkling of an eye**	im Nu, um Handumdrehen

My aunt is an excellent cook.
She can put a delicious meal on the
table in the twinkling of an eye.

~ **this day and age**	heutzutage
~-laws	die angeheirateten Verwandten
~s-and-outs	alle Einzelheiten

iron:

strike while the ~ is hot	das Eisen schmieden, solange es heiß ist
have too many ~s in the fire	zu viel auf einmal anpacken
~ s.th./things out	ein Problem lösen

It never rains but it pours. (Sprichw.) Ein Unglück kommt selten allein.

It's high time. Es ist höchste Zeit.

J

Jack/jack:

~ **of all trades** **(and masters of none)**	ein Hansdampf in allen Gassen
~ **is as good as his master.**	Wie der Herr, so's G'schärr.
~ **up s.o.** (am./Sl.)	jdn. motivieren

I guess I'll have to jack up the
workmen to do the job properly.

~ **up s.th.**	1. etwas mittels eines Hebers anheben, 2. Preis anheben

1. The mechanic jacked up the car
to look underneath.
2. The telephone company jacked up
the price of a call.

jam:

~ **the brakes on**	eine Vollbremsung machen
be in a ~	in der Patsche sitzen

job:
It's quite a ~. Es ist keine einfache Sache. Das ist nicht einfach.

make a good ~ of s.th. etwas ordentlich tun, gute Arbeit leisten

It isn't my ~. Das ist nicht mein Bier. Das geht mich nichts an.

jog:
~ **along** dahintrotten, weiterwursteln
~ **s.o.'s memory** jdm. auf die Sprünge helfen (geistig)

join:
~ **hands with** sich die Hände reichen
~ **up with s.o.** sich jdm. anschließen
~ **forces with s.o.** seine Kräfte mit denen einer anderen Person/Gruppe vereinigen

jump:
~ **the queue** sich vordrängeln
~ **to one's feet** aufspringen
~ **to conclusions** übereilte Schlüsse ziehen
~ **down s.o.'s throat** jdm. über den Mund fahren
~ **out of the frying pan into the fire** vom Regen in die Traufe kommen
(Sprichw.)

just:
my ~ right mein volles Recht
~ **in case** nur für den Fall
~ **one of those things** eine dieser unvermeidlichen Sachen
~ **what the doctor ordered** genau das Richtige

K

keep:
- **~ a civil tongue in one's head** — höflich reden/bleiben
- **~ a close watch on s.b.** — jdn. scharf beobachten
- **~ after s.b.** — jdn. verfolgen, jdm. nachstellen
- **~ an eye on s.o.** — jdn. im Auge behalten
- **~ at arms' length** — auf Distanz halten
- **~ s.th./s.o. at bay** — etwas/jdn. abwehren, fern halten

The soldiers managed to keep the enemy at bay.

- **~ at 1. s.o./2. s.th.** — 1. nörgeln, 2. bei etwas bleiben, darauf bestehen

1. *My mother keeps at me to go to university.*
2. *You'll never learn to play the piano unless you keep at it.*

- **~ company** — verkehren mit

A person is always judged by the company he keeps.

- **~ dark** — geheim halten

I'm leaving the firm next week, but please keep it dark.

- **~ one's fingers crossed** — die Daumen drücken
- **~ in check** — in Schranken halten, zügeln
- **~ in mind** — etwas nicht vergessen, an etwas denken
- **~ in ignorance** — in Unkenntnis lassen
- **~ in sight** — im Auge behalten
- **~ in touch with** — in Kontakt bleiben mit
- **~ on doing s.th.** — weiterhin etwas tun, fortfahren, etwas zu tun, etwas weiter tun
- **~ one's hand off s.th.** — die Finger von etwas lassen
- **~ one's head above water** — sich über Wasser halten (finanziell)
- **~ one's nose out of s.th.** — sich aus der Sache heraushalten
- **~ one's temper** — sich beherrschen
- **~ one step ahead of s.b.** — jdm. einen Schritt voraus sein
- **~ pace with** — Schritt halten mit
- **~ quiet** — ruhig bleiben, sich ruhig verhalten
- **~ s.o. company** — jdm. Gesellschaft leisten, bei jdm. bleiben
- **~ track of s.b.** — jdm. auf der Spur bleiben

~ **up with the times** mit der Zeit gehen, sich auf dem Laufenden halten
~ **your shirt on!** (Sl.) Hab Geduld! Warte einen Moment!

That's a pretty kettle of fish. (engl./Sl.) Das ist eine schöne Bescherung.

kick:
~ **a habit** (Sl.) sich etwas abgewöhnen
~ **over the traces** über die Stränge schlagen
~ **s.o. out** jdn. hinauswerfen
~ **the bucket** (Sl.) abkratzen, den Löffel abgeben

kill:
dressed to ~ aufgetakelt wie eine Fregatte
~ **s.o./s.th. off** jdm./etwas ein Ende bereiten
~ **time** die Zeit totschlagen
~ **two birds with one stone** zwei Fliegen mit einer Klappe schlagen
~ **with kindness** jdn. mit Freundlichkeit überhäufen

kiss:
~ **of death** der Todesstoß/-kuss
The judge's decision was the kiss of death for our plan.
~ **the dust** (Sl.) ins Gras beißen

knock:
~ **about** (Sl.) herumreisen
He spent his holiday knocking about in Scotland.
~ **it off!** (Sl.) Hör auf!
~ **out** bewusstlos schlagen
~ **s.o.'s block off** (Sl.) jdn. fest auf den Kopf schlagen
~ **up** 1. wecken, 2. schwängern

know:
~ **all the tricks of the trade** sich gut auskennen, gerissen sein
~ **a thing or two** (engl./Sl.) schlau sein, weise sein
~ **one's stuff** (Sl.) sich in seinem Fach gut auskennen
~ **s.th. inside out** etwas in- und auswendig kennen
~ **what's what** im Bilde sein
make ~n bekannt machen
~n all over the place (Sl.) bekannt wie ein bunter Hund

67

L

labour:
~ a point — etwas übermäßig betonen
I understand what you mean, you don't need to labour the point.
~ over s.th. — sich mit etwas abmühen
~ under a delusion — sich täuschen

lag behind — trödeln
Going for a walk with small children is no fun. They quickly lose interest and lag behind.

laid:
~ back (am./Sl.) — gelassen
~ up — 1. im Bett (krank), 2. außer Dienst (Reparatur)

1. *I've been laid up all week with a bad cold.*
2. *My car is laid up, it needs a new gearbox.*

land:
~ on one's feet — es gut treffen
~ s.b. in a mess — jdn. in Schwierigkeiten bringen
~ up as ... — als ... enden
see how the ~ lies — sich (diskret) erkundigen, die Lage sondieren

be at large — auf freiem Fuß sein

last:
~ but not least — und nicht zuletzt, und nicht zu vergessen
~ night — gestern Abend
of the ~ importance — von äußerster Wichtigkeit
the ~ but one — der Vorletzte
at long ~ — endlich
be on one's ~ legs — auf dem letzten Loch pfeifen
It's the ~ straw that breaks the camel's back (Sprichw.) — Es ist der Tropfen, der das Fass zum Überlaufen bringt.

late:
~ in life	im fortgeschrittenen Alter
her ~ husband	ihr verstorbener Ehegatte
of ~	in letzter Zeit
better ~ than never	lieber/besser zu spät als gar nicht

laugh:
~ **up one's sleeve** (Sl.)	sich ins Fäustchen lachen
have the last ~	das letzte Wort haben
~ **at s.b.**	jdn. auslachen
~ **s.th. off**	mit einem Lachen über etwas hinweggehen
~ **away s.o.'s fears**	die Angst von jdm. durch Lachen beschwichtigen
You'll ~ **on the other side of your face.**	Dir wird das Lachen schon noch vergehen.
He ~s best who ~s last. (Sprichw.)	Wer zuletzt lacht, lacht am besten.

rest on one's laurels — sich auf seinen Lorbeeren ausruhen

lay:
~ **aside one's worries**	seine Sorgen hinter sich lassen
~ **a trap for s.b.**	jdm. eine Falle stellen
~ **by for a rainy day**	einen Notgroschen beiseite legen
~ **claim to s.th.**	auf etwas Anspruch erheben
~ **down the law**	zeigen, wo es lang geht, herumkommandieren

The doctor laid down the law and told me to stay in bed.

~ **hold of s.th.** — etwas in die Hand nehmen, anpacken

69

~ **it on thick**   übertreiben
I don't believe half of what you say. You always lay it on thick.
~ **s.o. off**   jdn. entlassen
~ **plans**   Pläne machen
~ **on a party**   eine Party veranstalten
~ **one's cards on the table**   die Karten auf den Tisch legen
~ **s.th. on thick**   etwas dick auftragen
~ **stress on s.th.**   etwas betonen
~ **the blame for s.th. on s.b.**   jdm. die Schuld für eine Sache in die Schuhe schieben

lead:
~ **a dog's life**   ein Hundeleben führen
~ **astray**   auf den falschen Weg führen, fehlleiten
~ **off**   die Führung übernehmen, den Anfang machen
~ **on**   ermutigen, aufmuntern
~ **up the garden path**   jdn. an der Nase herumführen
~ **up to**   anleiten, überleiten zu, nach sich ziehen
~ **the life of Riley** (Sl.)   in Luxus leben

leaf:
~ **through**   durchblättern
turn over a new ~   eine neues Leben anfangen

leap at the chance   die Gelegenheit sofort wahrnehmen

learn:
~ **by heart**   auswendig lernen
~ **s.th. the hard way**   aus (bitterer) Erfahrung lernen
least said, soonest mended (Sprichw.)   Reden ist Silber, Schweigen ist Gold.

leave:
~ **alone**   in Ruhe lassen
~ **a lot to be desired**   sehr viel zu wünschen übrig lassen
~ **off**   aufhören, ablassen
~ **s.b. to himself/to his own devices**   jnd. sich selbst überlassen
~ **s.o. in the lurch**   jdn. im Stich lassen
~ **s.th. to chance**   etwas dem Zufall überlassen

~ word with s.o. eine Nachricht hinterlassen
take one's ~ seinen Abschied nehmen

lend:
~ s.b. hand jdm. zur Hand gehen
~ o.s. to s.th. sich zu etwas hergeben, bei etwas mitmachen

*This kind of plan is not one
I could lend myself to.*

length:
at great ~ lang und breit, ausführlich
at ~ nach einiger Zeit, mit der Zeit
At length, he got up and left the room.
go to any ~s über Leichen gehen
*He will go to any lengths
to get what he wants.*

let:
~ alone 1. nicht berühren, sich nicht einmischen 2. geschweige denn

1. *Let it well alone. That's none
   of our business.*
2. *I didn't ask Mary, let alone
   the rest of the family.*

~ grass grow under one's feet still stehen, nichts tun
*John is always busy, he doesn't let
the grass grow under his feet.*

~ off steam	Dampf ablassen, explodieren
~ **down**	1. enttäuschen, im Stich lassen,
	2. die Luft aus den Reifen lassen
~ **go!**	Lass los!
~ **it go at that**	es dabei bewenden lassen
~ **o.s. in for s.th.**	sich auf etwas einlassen
Let sleeping dogs lie. (Sprichw.)	Schlafende Hunde soll man nicht wecken.
~ **s.o. off the hook**	jdn. verschonen
~ **s.th. slide** (Sl.)	etwas vernachlässigen
~ **s.th. slip**	eine Bemerkung fallen lassen, etwas verraten
~ **the cat out of the bag**	ein Geheimnis lüften, die Katze aus dem Sack lassen

level:

do one's ~ best	sein Möglichstes tun
have/keep a ~ head	einen kühlen Kopf haben/behalten
on the ~	ehrlich
~ **with s.o.** (Sl.)	zu jdm. ehrlich sein

lie:

~ **down on the job**	nicht aufpassen, etwas schlecht erledigen

I have to keep an eye on the workmen, I don't want them lying down on the job.

~ **low** (Sl.)	sich ruhig und unauffällig verhalten
tell a ~	lügen, eine Lüge erzählen
~ **through one's teeth**	dreist lügen (überzeugend)
~ **at s.o.'s door**	für etwas verantwortlich sein
~ **in store for**	auf jdn. warten
a white ~	eine harmlose Lüge

life:

have the time of one's ~	etwas sehr genießen, eine wunderbare Zeit haben
not for the ~ of me	nicht um alles in der Welt
seek s.o.'s ~	jdm. nach dem Leben trachten
be the ~ and soul of the party	(der) Mittelpunkt des Festes sein
in the prime of ~	im besten Alter
as large as ~	in voller Größe

lift:

give s.b. a ~	jdn. (per Anhalter) mitnehmen

~ a hand against s.o.	jdm. Schläge androhen
not ~ a finger	keinen Finger rühren

light:

come to ~	aufgedeckt werden
His treachery only came to light after his death.	
in a good ~	günstig, in günstigem Licht
in the ~ of	in Anbetracht ...
~ upon	durch Zufall entdecken
make ~ a work of s.th.	ein anderes Licht auf etwas werfen
make ~ of	bagatellisieren
He always makes light of his disability.	
to see the ~	die Wahrheit erkennen, Erleuchtung erlangen (oft ironisch)

like:

and the ~	und Ähnliches
~ a bolt out of the blue (Sl.)	wie ein Blitz aus heiterem Himmel
~ a fish out of water	ungeschickt, fehl am Platz
~ it or lump it (Sl.)	Vogel friss oder stirb, eine Sache entweder akzeptieren/einsehen oder einfach hinnehmen
as ~ as two peas in a pod	wie ein Ei dem anderen
~ water off a duck's back	ohne sichtbaren Erfolg, ohne Eindruck zu machen
That's just ~ him.	Das sieht ihm ähnlich.
There is nothing ~ ...	Es geht nichts über ...

line:

be in ~ with	übereinstimmen mit
fall into ~ with s.b.	sich jdm. anschließen
~ up	sich anstellen
stand in ~	in einer Reihe stehen
take the ~ of least resistance	den Weg des geringsten Widerstandes gehen

live:

~ above/beyond one's means	über seine Verhältnisse leben
~ and let live	leben und leben lassen
~ on	sich ernähren von
~ through s.th.	etwas durchmachen
You have to ~ with it.	Du musst dich damit abfinden/ damit leben.

lock, stock and barrel alles, mit allem Drum und Dran
I finished the job at last, lock, stock and barrel.

long:
in the ~ run letztendlich
~ ago vor langer Zeit
~ time no see. (Sl.) Lange nicht gesehen!
~-standing lang geplant/ausgemacht
I have a long-standing invitation to a concert this evening.
~-suffering geduldig, ausdauernd
~-winded langatmig
~ for s.th. sich nach etwas sehnen
so ~ (Sl.) bis dann, später

look:
have a good ~ at s.th. sich etwas genau ansehen
~ s.o. in the eye jdm. ins Gesicht sehen
I don't like the ~ of it. Die Sache gefällt mir ganz und gar nicht.

it ~s like es sieht so aus, als ob
~ after s.b. sich um jdn. kümmern
~ ahead in die Zukunft blicken
~ daggers at s.o. (Sl.) jdn. böse anschauen

~ down on s.b. jdn. verachten
~ for suchen nach
~ forward sich freuen auf
~ for trouble (Sl.) Schwierigkeiten heraufbeschwören
~ here! Na hören Sie mal!
~ into s.th. einer Sache nachgehen
The headmaster promised to look into the matter.

~ **s.th. up**   etwas nachschlagen
~ **on s.b. as**   jdn. betrachten als, jdn. halten für
I look on him as a friend.
~ **out!**   Vorsicht! Pass auf!
~ **out for s.b.**   nach jdm. Ausschau halten
Look out for John
when you're in London.
~ **over s.th.**   etwas durchsehen
~ **the other way**   etwas absichtlich ignorieren
~ **up to s.o.**   zu jdm. aufblicken

loose:
on the ~ (Sl.)   ohne Bindung, auf der Suche nach Spaß/Abwechslung

at a ~ **end**   faul, untätig, ohne bestimmtes Ziel
have a ~ **tongue**   eine lose Zunge haben
lord it over s.o.   sich arrogant benehmen
The head of department
lords it over his assistants.

lose:
~ **face**   Einfluss/Ansehen verlieren, sich blamieren

~ **one's cool** (am./Sl.)   böse/wütend werden
~ **one's mind**   verrückt werden
~ **one's shirt** (Sl.)   alles verlieren
~ **one's temper**   wütend werden
~ **one's train of thought**   den Faden verlieren
~ **sight of**   aus den Augen verlieren
~ **touch with**   nicht mehr auf dem Laufenden sein, den Kontakt verlieren

lost in thought   in Gedanken verloren/vertieft

love:
fall in ~   sich verlieben
Give my ~ **to ...!**   Grüße bitte ... von mir.
~ **doing s.th.**   etwas sehr gerne tun
play for ~   nicht um Geld spielen
~ **at first sight**   Liebe auf den ersten Blick
no ~ **lost between**   sich nicht grün sein/mögen
not for ~ **or money**   überhaupt nicht, keineswegs
I've tried all the libraries, but I can't
find the book for love or money.

M

mad:
like ~ (Sl.)   wie verrückt
He's been playing tennis like mad all morning.
drive s.o. ~   jdn. verrückt machen
be ~ on/about s.o./s.th.   verrückt nach jdm. sein, etwas sehr gerne tun

go ~   wahnsinnig werden

make:
~ both ends meets   sich nach der Decke strecken
~ a deal with   ein Abkommen treffen mit
~ an example of s.b.   an jdm. ein Exempel statuieren
~ a fuss about s.th.   viel Aufhebens von/über etwas machen
~ a habit of s.th.   sich etwas zur Gewohnheit machen

~ a mountain out of a molehill   aus einer Mücke einen Elefanten machen
~ name for o.s.   sich einen Namen machen, bekannt werden
~ a song and dance of s.th.   ein fürchterliches Theater wegen etwas machen
~ do with s.th.   sich mit etwas behelfen
~ eyes at s.o.   jdm. schöne Augen machen
~ friends with   sich anfreunden
~ good money   gut verdienen
~ good use of s.th.   etwas richtig anwenden/einsetzen
~ haste!   Beeil dich!

~ one's way in the world	seinen Weg machen
~ peace	Frieden schließen
~ shift with	sich behelfen mit
~ s.th. a rule	sich etwas zur Regel machen
~ s.th. up	etwas erfinden, sich etwas ausdenken
~ s.th.	es schaffen, zu kommen (zu einer Einladung, Verabredung etc.)

We were sorry you couldn't come to the party but hope you'll make it next time.

~ the best of a bad job	gute Miene zum bösen Spiel machen
~ the grade	es schaffen, Erwartungen entsprechen
~ the most of one's life	sein Leben in vollen Zügen genießen, das Beste aus seinem Leben machen
~ **up for lost time**	verlorene Zeit wieder wettmachen
~ up one's mind	sich entschließen, eine Entscheidung treffen
~ one's way	vorankommen

many:

~ a one	manch einer
~ a long day	eine lange Zeit, eine Ewigkeit

We have not seen them for many a long day.

Tell that to the Marines! (Sl.)   Das mach' einem anderen weis.

matter:

what's the ~?	Was ist los?
as a ~ of fact	in der Tat
no ~ what	egal was
it doesn't ~	das macht nichts
~-of-fact	hart, geschäftsmäßig, ohne Gefühle
not mince ~s	kein Blatt vor den Mund nehmen

mean:

by all ~s	aber bitte sehr (als wohl wollende Zusage), unter allen Umständen
by no ~s	auf keinen Fall
~ well	es gut meinen

77

meet:
make ends ~	mit dem Geld auskommen

No matter how much I save, I don't seem to be able to make ends meet.

~ s.b.'s eye	den Blick erwidern
~ with an accident	verunglücken

mess:
be in a ~ (Sl.)	in der Tinte sitzen
~ about with s.th.	an etwas herumbasteln

a millstone round s.o.'s neck (Sl.)   ein Klotz am Bein

mind:
be in two ~s about s.th.	sich über etwas im Unklaren sein
give s.o. a piece of one's ~ (engl.)	jdm. gehörig die Meinung sagen
have s.th. in ~	etwas vorhaben, einen Plan haben
know one's ~	wissen, was man will
make up one's ~	sich entschließen
Never ~!	Das macht nichts!
read s.b.'s ~	jds. Gedanken lesen
speak one's ~	sagen, was man denkt
~ one's own business	sich um die eigenen Angelegenheiten kümmern
out of one's ~	wahnsinnig, von Sinnen

miss:
~ the mark	daneben liegen, falsch liegen
~ the train	den Zug verpassen
~ one's footing	ausrutschen, stolpern
~ the point	nicht verstehen, worum es geht

moment:
in a ~	bald, gleich
unguarded ~	ein Augenblick, in dem man nicht aufgepasst hat

money:
~ is no object.	Geld spielt keine Rolle.
pocket-~	Taschengeld

Get a move on!   Spute dich!

I'm not much of a ...   Ich bin kein großer ...

N

nail:
~ s.o. down — jdn. festnageln
I tried to nail him down as to the time of his arrival.

hard as ~s — sehr hart (von Menschen)

near:
~ at hand — in der Nähe, in Reichweite
a ~ thing — ein knappes Entkommen, gerade nochmal Glück haben

That was a near thing. You almost dropped that antique vase.
~ the mark — beinahe richtig
That wasn't quite the right answer but it was very near the mark.

neck:
~ and ~ — Kopf an Kopf
get it in the ~ (engl./Sl.) — bestraft werden

neither fish nor fowl — weder Fisch noch Fleisch

79

never mind! Lass gut sein, vergiss es!

the next but one der übernächste

no:
~ doubt sicher, ohne Zweifel
~ laughing matter eine ernste Sache

nose:
follow one's ~ immer der Nase nach
~ s.th. out etwas aufstöbern, aufdecken
turn one's ~ up at s.th. die Nase über etwas rümpfen
My cat turns up ist nose at tinned food, it only eats fresh meat.
under s.o.'s ~ vor der Nase von jdm.
~ around herumschnüffeln, Nachforschungen anstellen

not:
~ see wood for trees vor lauter Bäumen den Wald nicht sehen
~ born yesterday nicht von gestern
~ sleep a wink kein Auge zu tun

nothing:
~ of the kind absolut nichts, nichts dergleichen
~ to it einfach, leicht
~ to write home about (Sl.) nichts Aufregendes/Besonderes
I can make ~ of it. Damit kann ich nichts anfangen.
make ~ of a loss sich wegen eines Verlustes nicht ärgern

now:
~ and again hin und wieder
~ or never jetzt oder nie

make o.s. a nuisance lästig werden, zu einer Plage werden

a hard nut to crack eine harte Nuss

nuts:
drive s.b. ~ jdn. verrückt machen
~ about s.o. nach jdm. verrückt sein

O

be obliged to s.o. — jdm. sehr verbunden sein

occur to s.o. — jdm. einfallen

odd:
be at ~s with s.b. — mit jdm. auf Kriegsfuß stehen
The ~s are against you. — Du bist im Nachteil. Die Chancen stehen schlecht.

off:
~-hand — leichthin, lässig
~ duty — dienstfrei
~ limits — Zutritt verboten
~ the map — am Ende der Welt
~ the cuff — spontan, ohne Übung

pour oil on the flames — Öl ins Feuer gießen

on:
~ and off — gelegentlich
~ cloud nine (Sl.) — sehr glücklich, im siebten Himmel

~ edge — nervös
You can't have been sleeping well lately, you are so on edge.
~ one's toes — aufmerksam
~ second thoughts — nach reiflicher Überlegung

~ the spur of the moment (Sl.)	Hals über Kopf, plötzlich
~ the one hand	einerseits
~ the verge of	kurz davor sein ...
~ the wrong track	auf der falschen Fährte

once:
~ and for all	ein für alle Mal
~ in a while	gelegentlich

open:
~ and above board	offen und ehrlich
~ up to s.o.	mit jdm. offen reden

the other day — neulich

out:
~ cold	bewusstlos
~ and about	wieder unter den Menschen

I'm pleased to see you out and about after your illness.

~ and ~	gänzlich
~ of date	altmodisch
~ of all proportion	maßlos übertrieben
~ of print	vergriffen
~ of order	außer Betrieb, kaputt
~ of the corner of one's eye	aus dem Augenwinkel
~ of the frying pan, into the fire	aus dem Regen in die Traufe
~ of the woods (Sl.)	nicht mehr in der kritischen Phase
be ~	nicht zu Hause sein
have it ~ with s.o.	sich mit jdm. aussprechen
take it ~ on s.b.	etwas an jdm. auslassen

over:
all ~	aus und vorbei
~ and above s.th.	über etwas hinaus
~ and done with	aus und vorbei
~ one's head	zu hoch für jdn.

own:
hold one's ~	sich behaupten
on one's ~	allein, selbstständig
get one's ~ back	sich rächen
~ up to s.th.	sich zu etwas bekennen

P

pack:
~ **it in!** (Sl.) — Hör auf damit!
~ **s.o. off somewhere** — jdn. fortschicken, fortjagen
~**ed like sardines** — wie die Heringe, sehr eng
We were packed like sardines in the coach to London.
a ~ of lies — lauter Lügen
The story he told was nothing but a pack of lies.
~ **up** — aufhören, eine Aktion einstellen
We are wasting our time! We may as well pack up and go home.
send s.o. ~ing — jdn. kurzfristig entlassen

pain:
be a ~ in the neck (Sl.) — einem auf die Nerven gehen
take ~s to do s.th. — sich bei etwas große Mühe geben

paint:
~ **s.o. black** — jdn. als üblen Charakter darstellen
~ **the town red** — Radau machen, alles auf den Kopf stellen, feiern

pair off — paarweise gehen, zu zweit gehen

part:
~ and parcel of s.th.	ein wichtiger Bestandteil; alles; samt und sonders

A glittering tree, presents and good food are all part and parcel of Christmas.

for my ~	was mich betrifft
for the most ~	weitgehend, meistens
take ~ in	teilnehmen an
take s.b.'s ~	Partei ergreifen für jdn.
~ with s.o. or s.th.	sich von jdm. oder etwas trennen
be partial to	mögen, gern haben

I am rather partial to roast beef and yorkshire pudding.

pass:
~ away/on	sterben
~ a remark	eine Bemerkung machen
~ for	gelten als
~ off	1. vorgeben dass, 2. einen falschen Eindruck erwecken, 3. langsam weniger werden

1. *She disliked his bad matters, but tried to pass them off as a joke.*
2. *The girl liked to pass herself off as much older than she was.*
3. *A feeling of nausea overcame her, but it soon passed off.*

~ on	weitergeben
~ one's/the time	sich die Zeit vertreiben
~ out	ohnmächtig werden
~ over s.th./s.o.	über etwas/jdn. hinweggehen
~ the buck (Sl.)	jdm. den schwarzen Peter zuschieben
~ the time of day	jdm. „Guten Tag" sagen, jdn. grüßen

pay:
the devil to ~ (engl./Sl.)	ein fürchterlicher Aufruhr
~ attention	aufmerksam zuhören
~ back	1. zurückzahlen, 2. heimzahlen
~ s.o. a visit	jdn. besuchen
~ through the nose for s.th. (Sl.)	einen Haufen Geld für etwas bezahlen

~ one's way	aus dem Einkommen für die Ausgaben aufkommen

I don't think a business of this size will ever pay its way.

be as like as two peas in a pod (Sl.)	sich gleichen wie ein Ei dem anderen (siehe like)
take s.o. down a peg or two (Sl.)	jdm. einen Dämpfer verpassen
cost a pretty penny	eine hübsche Summe Geld kosten

pick:
~ **a quarrel with s.b.**	jdn. kritisieren, sticheln
~ **and choose** (engl.)	vorsichtig aussuchen
~ **holes in s.th./s.o.**	etwas/jdn. kritisieren
~ **on s.o./s.th.**	kritisieren, herumnörgeln
~ **one's way**	seinen Weg suchen
~ **one's words** (engl.)	sich vorsichtig ausdrücken
~ **out**	auswählen, herausfinden
~ **o.s. up**	wieder aufstehen, sich erheben, sich aufraffen
~ **s.b. up**	jdn. abholen, treffen
~ **s.th. up**	etwas aufschnappen

it's no picnic	Das ist kein Honigschlecken.
buy a pig in a poke (engl./Sl.)	die Katze im Sack kaufen

pile:
make one's ~ (engl./Sl.)	so viel Geld machen, wie man braucht
~ **it on (thick)**	übertreiben
~ **up**	sich anhäufen

pin:
~ **down**	festnageln, festmachen
~ **s.o.'s ears back** (am./Sl.)	jdn. schelten, schlagen
~ **up**	anstecken, feststecken

pipe:
~ **down!**	Red' nicht so viel!
put that in your ~ and smoke it (Sl.)	Das kannst du dir hinter die Ohren schreiben.
~ **up**	dazwischenreden, unterbrechen

pity:
What a ~! — Schade!
take ~ on — Mitleid empfinden für, jdm. helfen

place:
in the first ~ — erstens, zu allererst
in ~ of — anstelle von
out of ~ — nicht geeignet, Fehl am Platz

plain:
as ~ as the nose on your face (Sl.) — sonnenklar
~ speaking — offenes, ehrliches Sprechen (Meinung)
~ sailing — ohne Schwierigkeiten
be ~ with s.b. — mit jdm. offen reden

play:
~ ball — kooperieren
~ by ear — 1. nach Gehör spielen, 2. ohne festen Plan, den Umständen angepasst
bring s.th. into the ~ — ins Spiel bringen
~ for time — Zeit herausschinden
~ hooky (am./Sl.)/**~ truant** (engl.) — die Schule schwänzen
~ into s.o.'s hands — jdm. in die Hände spielen
~ one's cards well — die Gelegenheit ausnutzen
~ with fire — ein Risiko eingehen, mit dem Feuer spielen
~ed out — erschöpft, ausgebrannt

pocket:
put one's pride in one's pocket ~ — über seinen Schatten springen, klein beigeben
in one's ~ — unter Kontrolle
be out of ~ — finanzielle Verluste erleiden

point:
be on the ~ of doing s.th. — kurz davor sein, etwas zu tun
make a ~ of s.th. — auf etwas achten
He made a point of welcoming the late-comers very warmly.
~ out — hinweisen auf, hervorheben
stick to the ~ — bei der Sache bleiben, nicht abschweifen

come to the ~ zum Wesentlichen kommen
That's not the ~. Darum geht es nicht.
The ~ is that ... Die Sache ist die, dass ...
make a ~ zur Diskussion beitragen
a sore ~ ein wunder Punkt
My going out to work is a sore point with my husband.
strong ~ (typisches Merkmal) Stärke
Cleaning the house is not my strong point.
~ of view Meinung

poke:
~ fun at sich lustig machen über
~ one's nose into s.th. seine Nase in etwas stecken

pop:
~ in hereinplatzen, auf einen Sprung vorbeikommen

My neighbour is always popping in for a cup of tea.
~ the question (Sl.) einen Heiratsantrag machen

pot:
go to ~ (Sl.) ganz kaputt gehen
If you don't paint your fence soon it'll go to pot.

pour:
It never rains before it ~s. Ein Unglück kommt selten allein.
~ forth darauf los reden
~ cold water on s.th. dämpfend wirken
~ oil on troubled water beruhigen, schlichten, die Wogen glätten

press:
~ for pochen auf, bestehen auf
~ forward/on with vorankommen mit
prick up one's ears die Ohren spitzen

proof:
The ~ of the pudding is in the eating. (engl. Sprichw.) Probieren geht über Studieren.
put to the ~ testen

87

pull:
~ **a long face** (engl.)	ein langes Gesicht machen
~ **o.s. together**	sich zusammennehmen, zusammenreißen
~ **s.o.'s leg**	jdn. necken, foppen
~ **strings**	die Fäden aus dem Hintergrund ziehen, Beziehungen spielen lassen

It's easy to get a job if you have a rich uncle to pull strings.

push:
~ **one's luck**	weiterhin damit rechnen, dass alles gut geht

You've managed so far but don't push your luck.

~ **home**	nach Hause eilen
~**ing up daisies** (Sl.)	die Radieschen von unten wachsen sehen, tot sein

put:
~ **above all else**	vor alles andere stellen
~ **an end to s.th.**	einer Sache ein Ende bereiten
~ **by**	zurücklegen, beiseite legen, auf die hohe Kante legen
~ **in a (good) word for**	ein (gutes) Wort einlegen für
~ **ideas into s.o.'s head**	jdm. Flausen in den Kopf setzen
~ **in order**	in Ordnung bringen
~ **into the shade**	in den Schatten stellen
~ **into force**	in Kraft setzen
~ **into words**	in Worte fassen
~ **it down to ignorance**	etwas auf Unwissenheit zurückführen, als Dummheit auslegen

~ off one's stride	aus dem Tritt gebracht
~ on the shelf	an den Nagel hängen
~ on one's thinking cap	scharf nachdenken
~ on weight	zunehmen (Gewicht)
~ one foot before the other	einen Fuß vor den anderen setzen
~ one's heads together (Sl.)	die Köpfe zusammenstecken
~ o.s. in s.b.'s place	sich in jdn. hineinversetzen
~ **out of action**	außer Gefecht setzen
~ pressure on	Druck ausüben auf
~ s.o./s.th. across	jdn./etwas gut verkaufen, etwas vermitteln
~ s.b. off	1. aus der Fassung bringen, 2. jdm. absagen
~ s.b. on his guard	jdn. warnen
~ s.o. through the hoop(s)	jdn. einer schweren Prüfung unter ziehen
~ **s.th. right**	etwas richtig stellen
~ s.b. up	jdn. beherbergen
~ s.o. wise to s.th.	jdn. über etwas informieren, Bescheid geben
~ the lid on s.th.	etwas die Krone aufsetzen
~ the blame on s.b.	jdm. die Schuld in die Schuhe schieben
~ the cart before the horse	das Pferd von hinten aufzäumen
~ word into s.o.'s mouth	für jdn. ohne dessen Erlaubnis sprechen
~ two and two together	sich einen Reim machen auf
~ **up with s.th.**	sich etwas gefallen lassen

Q

quarter:
live in close ~s	eng beieinander wohnen
in all ~s	überall

a queer card   ein Exzentriker

question:
be out of the ~   außer Frage stehen, nicht in Frage kommen

beg the ~	auf eine Frage ausweichend reagieren, sich vor einer Entscheidung drücken
beyond all ~	ohne Frage, zweifellos
The ~ does not arise.	Die Frage stellt sich nicht.

quick:
~ on the draw	schlagfertig
~ on the uptake	von rascher Auffassungsgabe
cut to the ~	tief betroffen, verletzt

quiet:
on the ~	insgeheim, unter der Hand
~ down	sich beruhigen

quite:
~ so!	Ganz recht so!
~ a bit	ziemlich viel
~ a few	ziemlich viele
~ a number	eine beträchtliche Zahl
~ a lot	ziemlich viel/viele

R

race:
~ against time	Wettlauf mit der Zeit (auch als Verb)
The temperature is ~ing up	Die Temperatur steigt schnell.

rack:
~ one's brains	sich den Kopf zerbrechen
on the ~	äußerst gespannt, auf glühenden Kohlen

rain:
It's ~ing cats and dogs.	Es regnet Bindfäden.
save up for a ~y day	auf die hohe Kante legen

raise:
~ an objection (to)	einen Einwand erheben gegen
~ from the dead	jdn. von den Toten auferwecken

~ one's eyebrows	leicht schockiert sein
~ one's voice against s.th.	seine Stimme gegen etwas erheben

reach:

~ for the sky	hohe Ziele haben, nach den Sternen greifen
~ out for	greifen nach
out of ~	unerreichbar

read:

~ between the lines	zwischen den Zeilen lesen
~ into	hineinlesen
~ out	laut lesen
~ s.o. like a book	jdn. sehr gut kennen

red:

see ~	rot sehen
be in the ~	Schulden haben, in den roten Zahlen sein
like a ~ **rag to a bull**	wie ein rotes Tuch
see the ~ **light**	eine Warnung vor Schwierigkeiten erhalten

regard:

as ~**s me**	was mich betrifft
have no ~ **for**	nicht berücksichtigen, keine Rücksicht nehmen

remark:

pass a ~ **on**	sich äußern über
without ~	kommentarlos, stillschweigend

rein:
give ~ — die Zügel locker lassen
keep a tight ~ on — zügeln
My aunt is very strict and keeps at tight rein on her teenage son.
take the ~s — die Führung übernehmen
When her husband died Mary took the reins of the family business.

relieve:
~ one's feelings — seinen Gefühlen freien Lauf lassen

be reluctant to — etwas widerwillig tun

rest:
~ upon s.th. — sich auf etwas stützen
The responsibility ~s with you. — Du trägst die Verantwortung.
~ assured — zufrieden sein
~ on one's laurels — sich auf seinen Lorbeeren ausruhen

There's neither rhyme nor reason in that. — Das hat weder Hand noch Fuß.

ride:
~ one's hobby-horse — seinem Steckenpferd/Zeitvertreib nachgehen
take for a ~ — belogen, betrogen
take s.o. for a ~ — jdn. auf die Schippe nehmen

right:
by ~s — rechtens, nach dem Recht
put to ~ — berichtigen
you are ~ to do so — Du hast Recht, dich so zu verhalten.

~ away — sofort
serve s.o. ~ — jdm. recht geschehen
It serves you right if you are wet, you shouldn't have started splashing me.

ring:
give s.o. a ~ — jdn. anrufen
~ s.b. up — jdn. anrufen
~ off — ein Telefonat beenden
He was obviously offended, as he rang off without saying a word.

rip s.o. off (Sl.) — jdn. übers Ohr hauen

risk:
at one's own ~ — auf eigene Gefahr
run a ~ — ein Risiko eingehen
~ one's neck — Kopf und Kragen riskieren

roll:
~ up one's sleeves — die Ärmel hochkrempeln
The years ~ by. — Die Jahre vergehen.

When in Rome, do as the Romans do. (Sprichw.) — Im Ausland richtet man sich nach den örtlichen Gepflogenheiten.

room:
not ~ to swing a cat — so eng, dass man sich nicht umdrehen kann
~ for improvement — verbesserungsfähig, nicht ganz einwandfrei
~ with s.o. — mit jdm. eine Wohnung/Zimmer teilen

rope:
~ s.o. into (doing) s.th. — jdm. eine Arbeit aufhalsen
My brother roped me into helping him to move about the furniture.
know the ~s — die Spielregeln kennen

rough:
~ it primitiv leben
*When we go on holiday we don't
stay in hotels, we like to rough it.*
have a ~ time eine schwere Zeit haben

round:
a long way ~ ein Umweg
go ~ to s.b.'s jdn. besuchen
*I'm going round to Mary's
for the evening.*
~ off vollenden, fertig machen

rule:
as a ~ im Allgemeinen, generell
~ out ausschließen
~ing passion persönliche Vorliebe, Lieblings-
zeitvertreib

run:
~ a temperature Fieber haben
~ across zufällig begegnen
~ away with the idea sich einbilden
~ counter to im Widerspruch stehen
*This completely runs counter
to our plans.*
five days ~ning fünf Tage nacheinander
in the long ~ langfristig
in the short ~ kurzfristig
on the ~ auf der Flucht
~ out of ... keine ... mehr haben
*May I borrow some milk? I've run
out and want to bake a cake.*
~ over überfahren
~ short of s.th. etwas geht demnächst aus
*We are running short of time,
you have to hurry up.*
~ner-up der Zweite

rush:
~ one's fences etwas übers Knie brechen
~ into doing s.th. etwas überstürzt tun
~ s.o. to hospital jdn. schnellstens ins Krankenhaus
bringen

S

get the sack (engl./Sl.) — entlassen werden

safe:
be on the ~ side — um ganz sicher zu gehen
play it ~ — auf Nummer sicher gehen
~ and sound — gesund und munter

sake:
For God's ~! — Um Gottes willen!

What's sauce for the goose is sauce for the gander. — Was dem einen recht, ist dem anderen billig.

save:
~ s.b. from s.th. — jdn. vor etwas retten
~ the situation — die Lage retten
~ money — Geld sparen
~ up for (s.th.) — aufheben für, sparen für

say:
no sooner said than done — gesagt, getan
That goes without ~ing. — Das versteht sich von selbst.
that is to ~ — das heißt, vielmehr
when all is said and done — letzten Endes
~ s.th. in a roundabout way — etwas umständlich zum Ausdruck bringen
~ s.th. to s.o.'s face — jdm. etwas ins Gesicht sagen

scare:
be ~d stiff — zu Tode erschrocken sein, eine Heidenangst haben
~ s.o. to death — jdn. zu Tode erschrecken

scrape:
get into a ~ — in Schwierigkeiten geraten

screw:
put the ~ on s.b. — jdm. die Macht zeigen, jdn. zwingen
~ up one's courage — allen Mut zusammennehmen

search:
~ me! (Sl.)	Was weiß ich! Frag' mich etwas Leichteres!
in ~ of	auf der Suche nach
~ after	streben nach
make a ~ for	suchen nach

second:
on ~ thoughts	nach reiflicher Überlegung
~ sight	das zweite Gesicht

see:
~ with half an eye	sofort, auf einen Blick sehen
~ s.b. off	jdn. verabschieden
~ s.o. across the street	jdn. über die Straße bringen
~ s.b. home	jdn. nach Hause bringen
~ s.th. through	etwas zu Ende führen

seize:
be ~d with	ergriffen/befallen sein von
~ the opportunity	die Gelegenheit nutzen

sell:
~ at a loss	mit Verlust verkaufen
~ like hot cakes	sich wie warme Semmeln/Brötchen verkaufen
~ s.o. a pup	jdn. übers Ohr hauen

send:
~ for s.th.   nach etwas schicken
~ s.b. packing   jdn. fortjagen
~ word to s.o.   eine Nachricht schicken
I'll send word that we'll be catching the later train.

sense:
make ~   sinnvoll sein
make ~ of s.th.   etwas verstehen, begreifen
talk ~   vernünftig sein/reden

serve:
at your services   zu Ihren Diensten
~ as an excuse   als Entschuldigung dienen
~ its purpose   seinen Zweck erfüllen
That ~s them right.   Das geschieht ihnen recht.

set:
be hard ~   in großer Not sein
~ a dog on s.b.   einen Hund auf jdn. hetzen
~-back   Rückschlag
~ eyes on s.o./s.th.   etwas zum ersten Mal sehen
~ foot in   eintreten
~ in   beginnen, einsetzen
It looks as if winter will set in early this year.
~ one's heart on   sich etwas von Herzen wünschen
~ one's mind to   sich etwas in den Kopf setzen
~ to rights   in Ordnung bringen
~ up (shop)   (ein Geschäft) etwas aufbauen, einsetzen, ins Leben rufen

settle:
~ back   sich zurücklehnen
~ down   sich niederlassen, sesshaft werden, sich beruhigen
~ with s.o.   mit jdm. abrechnen
~ for s.th.   sich mit etwas zufrieden geben

shake:
~ hands   sich die Hand geben
~ in one's shoes   vor Angst zittern
~ s.o. up (Sl.)   jdn. schockieren, aufregen

shame:
~ on you! Schäm dich!
What a ~! Wie schade!

share:
have a ~ in teilhaben an
~ out among verteilen unter

That was a close shave. Das wäre beinahe ins Auge gegangen.

shed:
~ light on Licht werfen auf
~ tears over Tränen vergießen über

sheep:
a wolf in ~s clothing der Wolf im Schafspelz
cast ~'s eyes at verliebt/schmachtend ansehen

shift:
~ the responsibility on ... die Verantwortung auf ... schieben

shine:
make a ~ about Aufhebens machen um
take the ~ out of in den Schatten stellen
~ up to s.o. (am.) um die Gunst von jdm. bitten

It gives me the shivers. Es läuft mir kalt den Rücken herunter.

get the shock of one's life	sein blaues Wunder erleben

shoot:
~ **ahead**	schnelle Fortschritte machen
~ **a glance at**	einen raschen Blick werfen auf
~ **one's bolt**	seinen letzten Versuch machen

shot-gun wedding	Mussehe
shot in the dark	auf bloße Vermutung hin; ins Blaue hinein

shop:
~ **around**	einen Einkaufsbummel machen
talk ~	fachsimpeln

short:
run ~ **of**	knapp werden, etwas geht demnächst aus
~ **of cash**	knapp bei Kasse
cut s.o. ~	jdn. unterbrechen, jdm. über den Mund fahren
~ **-lived**	von kurzer Dauer

show:
~ **off**	angeben, prahlen
~ **up**	aufkreuzen

shut:
~ **down**	(endgültig) schließen
~ **one's eyes to s.th.**	die Augen vor etwas schließen
~ **up!** (Sl.)	Halt den Mund!
~ **the stable door when the horse has bolted**	den Brunnen zudecken, wenn das Kind ertrunken ist

I'm sick and tired of it.	Das hängt mir zum Hals raus.

side:
~ **against s.b.**	gegen jdn. Partei ergreifen
~ **by** ~	nebeneinander, einträchtig

sight:
at first ~	auf den ersten Blick
lose one's ~	erblinden
~ **for sore eyes**	ein willkommener Anblick

sink:
~ into oblivion	in Vergessenheit geraten, in der Versenkung verschwinden
~ into sleep	in tiefen Schlaf fallen

sit:
~ back and do nothing	die Hände in den Schoß legen
~ on the fence	zwischen zwei Stühlen sitzen
~ s.th. out	bis zum Ende bleiben, etwas aussitzen
~ tight (Sl.)	ausharren, geduldig warten
~ up for s.b.	für jdn. aufbleiben, auf jdn. warten

six:
~ of one and half a dozen	Jacke wie Hose, gehupft wie gesprungen
at ~es and sevens	durcheinander, konfus

by the skin of one's teeth — mit Hängen und Würgen, mit knapper Not

sleep like a log — schlafen wie ein Murmeltier

slip:
~ away	entwischen
~ into	hineinschlüpfen, sich hineinstehlen
~ s.th. on/over	sich etwas überziehen
~ through one's fingers	durch die Finger schlüpfen/rutschen
~ of the tongue	Versprecher
Freudian ~	Freud'scher Versprecher
give s.o. the ~	jdm. entkommen
~ up	Fehler machen

slow:
my watch is ~	meine Uhr geht nach
~(ly) but sure(ly)	langsam aber sicher

a smooth customer — ein ganz gerissener Kerl

That's the snag. — Da liegt der Hase im Pfeffer.

snap:
~ at s.b.	jdn. barsch anfahren

be sold down the river	verraten und verkauft
song:	
for a ~	für'n Appel und 'n Ei
make a ~ about	Aufhebens machen um
be in the soup	in der Patsche sitzen
call a spade a spade	das Kind beim rechten Namen nennen
throw a spanner in the works	jmd. einen Knüppel zwischen die Beine werfen

speak:	
~ of the devil (and he appears).	Wenn man vom Teufel spricht, kommt er.
generally/roughly ~ing	im Großen und Ganzen, grob gesagt
not to ~ of	ganz zu schweigen von
so to ~	sozusagen
~ one's mind	die Meinung sagen
~ up	lauter reden
spick and span	sehr ordentlich, geschniegelt und gebügelt
cry over spilt milk	über Dinge jammern, die nicht mehr zu ändern sind
spin:	
~ out	in die Länge ziehen
be the spitting image of s.o.	jdm. wie aus dem Gesicht geschnitten sein

be born with a silver spoon in one's mouth — reich auf die Welt kommen

spot:
a ~ of — etwas (von), ein wenig
be on the ~ — zur Stelle sein

stamp:
a man of that ~ — ein Mann dieses Schlages
set one's ~ on — seinen Stempel aufdrücken

stand:
make a ~ — sich widersetzen
~ a chance — eine Chance haben
~ by — bereitstehen
~ for — repräsentieren, stehen für
~ in for s.o. — jdn. vertreten
~ together — zusammenhalten
~ up for — eintreten für
~ s.o. up — jdn. sitzen lassen
~ well with s.o. — mit jdm. gut stehen
It ~s to reason. — Es ist ganz klar und logisch.

start:
to ~ with — zunächst einmal
That gave him a ~. — Das ließ ihn zusammenzucken/zusammenfahren.

steal:
~ away — sich davonstehlen

step:
~ in — einschreiten, unterbrechen
~ on the gas — Gas geben, sich beeilen
~ out of line — aus der Reihe tanzen

stick:
~ to the point — bei der Sache bleiben
~ by s.o. — jdm. treu bleiben, unterstützen
~ one's neck out (Sl.) — ein Risiko eingehen
~ s.th. out — etwas aushalten, etwas durchstehen

stop:
~ dead — plötzlich stehen bleiben

~ off	Zwischenstation einlegen
We are going to stop off in Salzburg on the way to Vienna.	
~ by (am./Sl.)	vorbeischauen

store:
be in ~ for s.b.	jdm. bevorstehen
set great ~ by	Wert legen auf

a storm in a teacup	ein Sturm im Wasserglas

straight:
~ ahead	geradeaus
~ away/off	sofort
~-forward	schlicht, einfach, geradeheraus

straw:
the ~ that breaks the camel's back	der Tropfen, der das Fass zum Überlaufen bringt
clutch at (a)~(s)	sich an einem Strohhalm festklammern

stretch one's legs	sich die Beine vertreten

strike:
~ at the root of	an der Wurzel treffen
~ a happy medium	zu einem Kompromiss kommen
~ while the iron is hot	das Eisen schmieden, solange es heiß ist

stuff:
made of the same ~	aus dem gleichen Holz geschnitzt
~ and nonsense!	Unsinn!

subject:
~ to this unter diesem Vorbehalt
~ to change Änderungen vorbehalten

such:
~ is life. So ist das Leben.
no ~ thing nichts dergleichen
Suit yourself. Mach, wie du meinst.

swallow:
~ one's pride über seinen Schatten springen, klein beigeben
~ the pill (Sl.) in den sauren Apfel beißen
~ an insult eine Beleidigung hinnehmen

swear:
~ at s.b. auf jdn. fluchen
~ in vereidigen

be in a cold sweat (Sl.) Blut und Wasser schwitzen

sweep:
make a clean ~ reinen Tisch machen
~ across one's mind einem in den Sinn kommen

T

to a ~ genau
This description is correct to a T.

be on the wrong track auf dem Holzweg sein

tail:
~ after s.b. jdm. hinterherlaufen
~ between his legs wie ein erschrockener Hund, mit eingezogenem Schwanz

take:
~n aback überrascht
~ a beating Prügel beziehen

~ **the bull by the horns** (engl.)	den Stier bei den Hörnern packen
~ **after s.o.**	nach jdm. geraten
~ **a fancy to s.b**	sich vernarren in, eine Vorliebe entwickeln für
~ **for granted**	als Tatsache hinnehmen, voraussetzen

~ **in good/bad part** — in guter/schlechter Laune etwas hinnehmen

He usually takes my advice in good part.

~ **heart**	sich ein Herz fassen
~ **hold of s.th.**	etwas ergreifen
~ **in**	irreführen, betrügen

We were completely taken in by his story.

~ **it from me.**	Sie können mir glauben.
~ **note of**	notieren, festhalten
~ **notice of**	beachten
~ **offence at**	Anstoß nehmen an
~ **one's hat off to s.b.**	vor jdm. den Hut ziehen
~ **one's leave**	sich verabschieden
~ **one's life in one's own hands**	die Verantwortung für sich selbst übernehmen
~ **one's life**	Selbstmord begehen
~ **s.b.'s life**	jdn. töten
~ **one's time**	sich Zeit lassen
~ **pity on**	sich erbarmen, jdm. helfen
~ **revenge**	sich rächen
~ **s.b. at his word**	jdn. beim Wort nehmen
~ **s.b's breath away**	jdm. den Atem verschlagen

She was so beautiful it took my breath away.

~ s.o. for s.o.	jdn. mit jdm. verwechseln
~ s.th. at face value	etwas für bare Münze nehmen
~ s.th. out on s.o.	etwas (Ärger etc.) an jdm. auslassen
~ s.b.'s mind off s.th.	jdn. von etwas ablenken
~ things as they come	die Dinge auf sich zukommen lassen
~ to one's heels	die Beine in die Hand nehmen
~ turns at	sich abwechseln mit
What do you ~ me for?	Wofür halten Sie mich denn?

talk:

have a ~ with s.o.	sich mit jdm. unterhalten
~ about	reden über
~ back	frech antworten

How many times have I told you that it is rude to talk back at your elders?

~ down to s.o.	herablassend zu jdm. sprechen, sich einfach ausdrücken
~ shop	(zu unpassenden Gelegenheiten) über Berufliches reden
~ s.o. down	jdn. im Gespräch überzeugen, jdn. überreden
~ s.o. into doing s.th.	jdn. zu etwas überreden
~ s.o. out of s.th.	jdm. etwas ausreden
~ s.o.'s head off (Sl.)	zu viel reden
~ s.o. round	jdn. überreden
~ round s.th.	drumherum reden
~ until one is blue in the face (Sl.)	bis man schwarz wird, bis zur Erschöpfung reden

tear:

~ away from	sich losreißen
~ down	abreißen
~ one's hair	ängstlich, nervös oder wütend sein
~ to pieces	in Stücke reißen

The critics tore the performance of Hamlet to pieces.

tell:

~ apart	auseinander halten, unterscheiden
~ on s.o.	jdn. verraten, verpetzen
~ s.o. off	mit jdm. schimpfen
~ tales	flunkern

temper:
have a quick ~ heftig sein, schnell in Wut geraten
He has such a quick temper, every discussion ends in an argument.
keep one's ~ sich nicht aus der Ruhe bringen lassen

lose one's ~ die Beherrschung verlieren

terms:
be on bad ~ with sich schlecht verstehen mit
come to ~ with sich einigen mit, sich auf ... einstellen

on equal ~ zu gleichen Bedingungen, auf gleiche Weise

test:
put to the ~ auf die Probe stellen
stand the ~ bestehen, sich bewähren
The old car stood the test and finished the race without breaking down.

He won't set the Thames on fire. Der reißt keine Bäume aus.

thank:
~ goodness/heaven Gott sei Dank
~s to dank, wegen

thick:
a bit ~ (engl./Sl.) leicht unverschämt
To expect me to pay all your bills is a bit thick.
in the ~ of im dichtesten ..., mittendrin
We were suddenly caught up in the thick of the crowd.
~-skinned dickfellig
through ~ and thin durch dick und dünn

thing:
have a ~ about (engl./Sl.) besessen sein von
just the ~/the very ~ genau das Richtige

think:
~ better of s.th. einen schon gefassten Entschluss ändern

107

~ fit   beschließen, für angemessen erachten (oft ironisch)

The young man, having neither a job nor any money, thought fit to get married.

~ highly of   bewundern, viel von jdm. halten

He's a thorn in my side/flesh.   Er ist mir ein Dorn im Auge.

thought:
A penny for your ~s!   Woran denkst du?
on second ~s   nach reiflicher Überlegung

thread:
lose the ~   den Faden verlieren
The professor lost the thread in the middle of his lecture.
 pick up the ~   wieder anfangen (nach Unterbrechung)

throw:
~ away   durch Nachlässigkeit verlieren, wegwerfen
~ in   hinzufügen, einwerfen
~ light on   Licht werfen auf
~ open   eröffnen, aufreißen (Tür)
~ one's money about   mit Geld um sich werfen
~ o.s. into work   sich in die Arbeit stürzen
~ o.s. at s.o.   sich jdm. an den Hals werfen
~ s.o. off balance   jdn. aus dem Gleichgewicht bringen
~ s.o. over   jdm. den Laufpass geben
~ up   sich übergeben

tickle:
~d to death (Sl.)   äußerst amüsiert
~ s.o.'s fancy   jdn. interessieren, neugierig machen

time:
ahead of ~   früher als erwartet
before one's ~   vor jms. Zeit, bevor man geboren wurde
from ~ to ~   dann und wann

once upon a ~ Es war einmal ...
pressed for ~ sehr unter Zeitdruck
race against ~ Wettlauf mit der Zeit
~ after ~ ; ~ and ~ again immer wieder

today of all days ausgerechnet heute

toe:
~ the line sich den Regeln/dem Druck beugen
The Prime Minister expects her cabinet to toe the line.
tread on s.o.'s ~s jdm. auf den Schlips treten

tongue:
hold one's ~ den Mund halten, schweigen
be on the tip of one's ~ auf der Zungenspitze liegen
~ in cheek ironisch

touch:
get in ~ with sich in Verbindung setzen mit
~ wood auf Holz klopfen

treat:
It is my ~. Das geht auf meine Rechnung.
~ s.b. to s.th. jdm. etwas spendieren, mit etw. verwöhnen

trouble:
ask/look for ~ Ärger suchen
take the ~ sich die Mühe machen

true:
come ~ — sich bewahrheiten
be ~ of — zutreffen auf
be ~ to s.b. — jdm. treu sein
show one's ~ colours — sein wahres Gesicht zeigen

try:
~ one's hand at — versuchen, seinen ersten Versuch machen

John tried his hand at cooking while Mary was away.
~ s.o.'s patience — die Geduld von jdm. auf die Probe stellen

turn:
~ a deaf ear to — sich taub stellen
~ in — ins Bett gehen
~ inside out — das Innere nach außen kehren
~ one's back on s.b. — jdm. den Rücken zuwenden, sich von jdm. abwenden

He turned his back on me to indicate his displeasure.
~ on s.b. — vor jdm. davonlaufen
~ wagging the dog — das Unwichtige maßgebend sein lassen
~ out to be — sich herausstellen als/dass
~ over a new leaf — ein neues Leben beginnen, von vorn anfangen
~ s.b.'s brain/head — jdm. den Kopf verdrehen
~ s.th. upside down — das Unterste zuoberst kehren
~ tail — abhauen
~ the tables — den Spieß umdrehen
~ to one's advantage — etwas zu seinem Vorteil wenden
~ up — aufkreuzen, erscheinen

twiddle one's thumbs — Zeit verschwenden, Däumchen drehen

twist:
~ s.o.'s arm — jdn. unter Druck setzen
I had to twist his arm a little, but he finally came out with the full story.
~ s.o. round one's little finger — jdn. um den kleinen Finger wickeln

U/V

as ugly as sin — hässlich wie die Nacht

be unaware of s.th. — sich einer Sache nicht bewusst sein, etwas nicht merken

under:
come ~ — klassifiziert werden als
~ the counter — illegal (gekauft/verkauft), unter der Hand

~ the weather (Sl.) — unpässlich, krank
John isn't coming to work today, he is feeling under the weather.

unfit for — nicht geeignet sein, nicht fähig zu

up:
~ in arms — empört
She was up in arms about the way everybody had been treating her.
~s and downs — Höhen und Tiefen
~ and about — (wieder) gesund und munter
Mary was ill for a while, but now she is up and about again.
~ against s.th. — in Schwierigkeiten stecken, vor einem Problem stehen

be ~ to s.th. — einen Plan aushecken, bevorstehen, etwas zu tun

~ to it — in der Lage sein, etwas zu tun
You can't expect him to do that, he is simply not up to it.
It's ~ to you. — Das liegt bei dir.

use:
make ~ of — verwenden, ausnutzen
~ one's head — den Verstand gebrauchen
~ s.th. up — etwas aufbrauchen
~d to s.th. — an etwas gewöhnt sein
It's no ~. — Es hat keinen Zweck.

vain:
in ~ — vergeblich
take in ~ — leichtfertig mit etwas umgehen

111

vanish into thin air — sich in Luft auflösen

with velvet gloves — sanft

verge:
be on the ~ of doing s.th. — im Begriff sein, etw. zu tun
be on the ~ of madness — am Rande des Wahnsinns stehen

view:
bird's-eye ~ — Vogelperspektive
in my ~ — meiner Meinung nach
in ~ of — angesichts
take a long ~ — langfristig planen

virtue:
by ~ of — aufgrund, infolge
make a ~ of necessity — aus der Not eine Tugend machen

voice:
at the top of one's ~ — so laut wie möglich
give ~ to — zum Ausdruck bringen
raise one's ~ — lauter werden, schreien
the ~ of reason — die Stimme der Vernunft
with one ~ — einstimmig

W

wait:
keep s.b. ~ing — jdn. warten lassen
lie in ~ — auf der Lauer liegen
~ and see — abwarten

walk:
~ all over s.o. — jdn. sehr schlecht behandeln
~ off with — sich davonmachen mit
~ on air — glücklich sein
~ out on s.b. — jdn. verlassen, im Stich lassen

want:
for ~ of — mangels
~ s.th. badly — etwas unbedingt wollen

war:
be at ~ with — im Krieg liegen mit
be in the ~s — angeschlagen sein, mitgenommen aussehen

wash:
~ one's hands of s.th. — seine Hände in Unschuld waschen

waste:
~ away — dahinsiechen
~ one's breath — Zeit verschwenden, umsonst reden

water:
be in low ~ — auf dem Trockenen sitzen
fish in troubled ~s — im Trüben fischen

in hot ~ — in Schwierigkeiten
make s.b.'s mouth ~ — jdm. den Mund wässrig machen
Still ~s run deep. (Sprichw.) — Stille Wasser gründen tief.

way:
by the ~ — übrigens
get into the ~ of — sich angewöhnen zu
You will soon get into the way of using the computer.
have one's ~ — seinen Willen durchsetzen
pave the ~ for — den Weg bereiten für

wear:
~ s.th. down/out — abnutzen, verbrauchen
~ on — sich dahinschleppen
The evening wore on and the guests were getting restless.
~ and tear — Abnutzung

weigh:
~ **s.o. down**	jdn. belasten, bedrücken
~ **on one's mind**	beschäftigen, belasten
~ **one's words**	seine Worte abwägen, bedenken
~ **up**	einschätzen, beurteilen

He is a difficult person to weigh up.

have a whale of a time   eine tolle Zeit haben

what:
I tell you ~.   Ich mach dir einen Vorschlag.
I tell you what let's go to the cinema.

wild:
~ **goose chase**	ein sinnloses Unterfangen
~ **guess**	blinde Vermutung
~ **horses wouldn't make me do it.**	Keine zehn Pferde bringen mich dazu.
run ~	wild wachsen, verwildern

will:
against s.o.'s ~	gegen den Willen von jdm.
Where there is a ~ there is a way.	Wo ein Wille ist, ist auch ein Weg.

wind:
get ~ of	spitz kriegen, in Erfahrung bringen
like the ~	schnell wie der Wind
put the ~ up s.o. (Sl.)	jdm. Angst einjagen
see which way the ~ blows	sehen, wie der Hase läuft
take the ~ out of s.o.'s sails	jdm. den Wind aus den Segeln nehmen

wit:
be at one's ~s ends	mit seinem Latein am Ende sein
keep one's ~s about one	seine fünf Sinne beisammen halten
out of one's ~s	von Sinnen (sein)

within:
I was within an ace of being run down by the van.
~ **an ace of**	beinahe
~ **easy reach**	leicht erreichbar

pull the wool over s.o.'s eyes   jdm. Sand in die Augen streuen

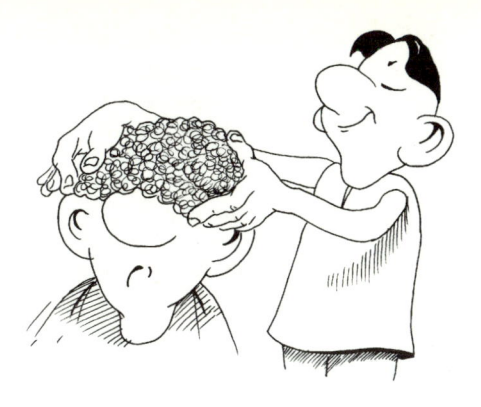

word:
be as good as one's ~	sein Wort halten
by ~ of mouth	mündlich
have the last ~ in s.th.	das letzte Wort haben

work:
make short ~ of	schnell beenden
~ upon	einwirken auf
~ one's way up	sich hocharbeiten
~ out	1. ausrechnen, 2. planen, 3. kosten, 4. Sport treiben

1. *The architect worked out how many apartment could be built on the site.*
2. *We'll work out the details of our holiday trip later.*
3. *The cost works out at 5 pounds a head.*
4. *He used to be overweight, but since he has taken to working out regularly, he has lost twenty kilograms.*

~ wonders	Wunder wirken

wrap:
~ped up in	vollständig in Anspruch genommen von

He is wrapped up in his family.

write:
nothing to ~ home about	nichts besonderes
~ off	etwas abschreiben

Y

year:
~ in, ~ out — Jahr für Jahr
all the ~ round — das ganze Jahr über

yearn for — sich sehnen nach

yell out — hinausschreien
He yelled out when the horse trod on his foot.

not yet — noch nicht

yield:
~ place to — Platz machen für
~ the right-of-way — jdm. die Vorfahrt lassen
~ to despair — sich der Verzweiflung hingeben
~ up s.th. — etwas aufgeben

Z

zap (Sl.) — schnell irgendwohin flitzen
I'll just zap down to the supermarket and get some snacks.
zero in on s.th. — etwas anpeilen, genau ansprechen

zip:
~ along — schnell fahren

Register

A

A und O 12
abblasen 21
abfinden 20, 73
abgewöhnen 53, 67
abhauen 25, 26
abholen 21, 85
Abkommen 76
abkratzen 67
abkühlen 29
Abkürzung 30
ablenken 106
abmachen 33
abmühen 68
abnutzen 113
abrechnen 97
abreißen 106
absagen 89
Abschied 71
abschreiben 115
abwarten 23, 112
abwechseln 106
Abwechslung 75
achten 59, 86
ächten 29
ähnlich 73
Ahnung 26, 37
Alkohol 53
alles in allem 7
Allüren 6
Alter 64, 69, 72
altmodisch 82
Amen 39
amüsiert 108
Anblick 99
andererseits 54
Änderung 18
Änderungen 104
Anerkennung 49
anfahren 100
Anfang 10, 29, 46, 70
anfangen 40, 80, 108, 110
anfreunden 76
angeben 99
Angelegenheit(en) 20, 50, 54, 78
angemessen 108
Angst 46, 58, 69, 97, 114
Anhalter 72
anhäufen 85
anheben 64
anpacken 57, 64, 69
anpeilen 116
anrechnen 24
anrufen 22, 47, 93,
anschauen 49, 74
anscheinend 8, 41
anschreiben lassen 24
Anspruch 115
anstelle von 86
anstellen 73
Anstoß 105
Antrieb 4
anwenden 76
Apfel 25, 52, 104
Apparat 60
Appel 101
Applaus 19, 47
Arbeit 10, 38, 41, 65, 93, 108
Ärger 109
Ärmel 93
Armut 46
arrogant 58
Asse 59
Ast 15
Atem 23, 105
Atemzug 36
auf allen vieren 7
aufatmen 4
aufbleiben 100
aufblicken 75
aufdrängen 62
auferwecken 90
Auffassungsgabe 90
aufführen 22
aufgeben 116
aufgedeckt 73
aufgeregt 61, 62
aufgetakelt 36, 67
aufgrund 5, 112
aufhalsen 93
aufheben 95
Aufhebens 41, 46, 76, 98, 101
aufheitern 24
aufholen 46
aufhören 16, 50, 67, 70, 83
aufkreuzen 99, 110
aufmerksam 81, 84
Aufmerksamkeit 23, 36
aufpassen 72, 78
aufraffen 85
aufräumen 25

117

aufregen 97
aufregend 30
Aufregendes 80
aufreißen 108
Aufruhr 84
aufschnappen 85
aufspielen 49
aufspringen 65
aufstöbern 34, 80
(auf)tanken 47
Auge(n) 13, 16, 22, 26, 30, 37, 38, 40, 63, 66, 75, 76, 80, 98, 99, 108, 114
Auge in Auge 41
Augenwinkel 82
aus und vorbei 32
Ausdruck 112
ausdrücken 85, 106
auseinander-setzen 47
ausführlich 10, 71
ausgebrannt 86
ausgerechnet 109
aushalten 4, 102
ausharren 100
auskennen 67
auskommen 35, 47, 78
auslachen 69
ausreden 58, 106
Ausschau 75
außer Betrieb 82
äußern 91
aussitzen 100
aussprechen 82
aussuchen 85
ausverkauft 25
ausweinen 30
auswendig 70

B

babyleicht 9
bagatellisieren 73
bald 14, 32, 78
bar 106
Bäume 80, 107
beachten 105
bedienen 58
Bedingung(en) 28, 36, 38, 107
bedrücken 114
beenden 93, 115
befallen 96
befassen 33
befreien 38
begegnen 19
Begeisterung 27
begreifen 97
Begriff 112
behaupten 4, 52, 60
behelfen 76, 77
beherbergen 89
beherrschen 53, 56, 59, 66
beherrscht 9
Beherrschung 44, 107
behilflich 58
Beine 4, 45, 57, 58, 101, 103, 106
beiseite 88
bekannt 67, 76
bekannt machen 67
bekennen 82
Belangloses 40
Beleidigung 104
Bemerkung 15, 72, 84
benehmen 6
bequem 38, 60
Berg 37
berichtigen 93
berücksichtigen 7, 91

beruhigen 29, 34, 87, 90
beschäftigt 9
Bescheid 89
Bescherung 67
beschimpfen 21
beschwichtigen 69
Besen 56
besessen sein 107
Besitz 60
Besitzer 24, 54
besser 32, 52
besser machen 51, 62
Beste(s) 12, 35, 49, 60, 77
Besten 14, 46
bestenfalls 14
bestraft 79
besuchen 21, 84
beteiligen 29
betonen 68, 70
betrifft 9, 91
betrogen 92
betrügen 105
betrunken 54, 63
Bett 59, 110
beugen 109
bevorstehen 103, 111
bewaffnen 8
bewähren 107
bewahrheiten 60, 110
bewandert 52
bewenden lassen 72
bewundern 108
bewusst machen 11
bewusstlos 82
Beziehungen 88
Biegen und Brechen 21, 60
Bier 65
Bilanz 12
billig 20, 95

Bindfäden 91
Binsen 35
bis dann 74
blamieren 75
Blatt 77
Blick 31, 41, 43, 49, 50, 75, 78, 96, 99
Blitz 12, 17, 73
blitzschnell 16
Blut 16
Blut und Wasser 104
Boden 19, 52, 57
böhmische Dörfer 52
böse 28, 49, 74
Botschaft 58
brauchen 11
brechen 94
bringen 96
Brücken 19
Brunnen 99
Buch 17

C

Chance 24, 81, 102
Chaos 56
Charakter 83
Chef 24

D

Dach und Fach 12
dahinschleppen 36, 113
dahinsiechen 113
Dampf 16, 48, 72
Dämpfer 85
dank 107
dann und wann 40, 108
Dauer 99
Däumchen 110
Daumen 30, 66
davonkommen 56
davonlaufen 110
davonstehlen 102
dazwischen 14
Decke 50, 51, 76
demütigen 38
deprimiert 16, 58
deutlich 26, 44
dicht hinterher 55
dick auftragen 70
dick und dünn 107
dickfellig 107
dienen 97
Diensten 97
dienstfrei 81
Dinge 8, 106
Diskussion 87
diskutieren 24
Distanz 8, 34, 65
Dorn 108
dringend brauchen 11
Druck 89, 109, 110
drücken 30, 89
drum und dran 74
drumherum reden 106
dumm 55
dumm und dusselig 57
durchblättern 70
durchboxen 39
durcheinander 10, 61, 62, 100
durchhalten 55
durchmachen 73
durchsehen 75
durchsetzen 57, 113
durchstehen 102
Durst 39
Dutzend 21

E

Ecke 19, 36
egal 45
Ehegatte 69
Ehre 42, 49
Ehren 59
Ehrensache 60
Ehrenschulden 60
ehrlich 4, 36, 51, 72, 82, 86
Ei 45, 73, 85, 101
Eile 61
eilen 88
ein für alle Mal 47, 82
einbilden 94
einbläuen 54
Eindruck 73, 84
einerseits 82
einfallen 81
eingeschnappt 62
eingraben 34
einhämmern 37
Einkaufsbummel 99
einlassen 40, 72
einmischen 60
einnicken 37
einstellen 34, 107
einstimmig 112
eintreten für 102
Einwand 7, 90
Einzelheiten 64
Eis 62
Eisen 57, 64, 103
Elefant 14, 19, 76
empört 111
Ende 7, 28, 29, 36, 40, 50, 67, 81, 88, 96, 100, 114
enden 40, 68
endlich 10, 63, 68
eng 54, 83

engagieren 40
Enge 11
entkommen 47, 100
Entkommen 79
entlassen 48, 70, 83, 95
entscheiden 33
Entscheidung 22, 54, 77, 89
entschließen 77, 78
entschlossen 45
entsprechen 8, 77
enttäuschen 31, 72
entwischen 47, 100
erbarmen 105
erblinden 99
ereignen 27
Erfahrung 54, 114
erfinden 77
Erfolg 41, 73
erfolgreich 22
erfüllen 97
erhalten 91
erheben 69, 85, 90
erklären 4, 19
erkranken 27
Erlaubnis 89
erledigen 4, 31, 33
erledigt 9
erleichtern 38
ermutigen 39, 70
ernähren 73
ernst 41, 80
erraten 43
erreichbar 114
erschöpft 32, 86
erschrecken 49, 95
Erwartungen 77
es war einmal 109
essen 34, 39, 57
Eulen 22
Ewigkeit 77

Exempel 76
Exzentriker 89

F

fachsimpeln 99
Faden 55, 75, 108
Fäden 88
Fährte 82
Fall 10, 21, 23, 32, 65, 77
Falle 23, 69
falls 23
falsch liegen 12, 78
fälschen 28
Farbe 27
Fassung 89
fast 7
Faust 60
Fäustchen 9
federleicht 43, 73, 86
fehl am Platz 42, 73, 86
Fehler 100
fehlleiten 70
Feierabend 21, 26, 32
Feindschaft 31
fertig 9
festhalten 105
festnageln 79, 85
feststecken 85
Fettnäpfchen 37
Feuer 81, 86
Fieber 94
finden 24, 27, 34
Finger 43, 48, 54, 66, 73, 100, 110
Fisch 44, 79
fit 27
Flasche 29
Flausen 62, 88

Fliegen 15, 67
fluchen 104
Flucht 94
flunkern 106
foppen 88
fortjagen 83, 97
Fortschritte 99
Frage 89
frech 8, 106
freien Lauf 92
freuen 25, 74
Frieden 77
früher 6, 108
Fuchs und Hase 64
Führung 57, 70, 92
fünf vor zwölf 39
Fuß 45, 48, 68, 89, 92
Fußstapfen 45

G

G'schärr 64
Gänsehaut 48
ganz und gar 74
gänzlich 82
Gas 102
Gaul 35
geborgen 9
Gedächtnis 22
Geduld 67, 110
geduldig 74, 100
Gefahr 56, 93
Gefallen 42
gefällig 38
Gefecht 89
Gefühl(e) 42, 43, 61, 92
gegen den Strich 50
Gegenwart 58
geheim 31, 66

Geheimnis 23, 49, 57, 72
geheuer 43
Gehör 38, 86
gehupft wie gesprungen 19, 100
Geige 43
geistesabwesend 57, 62
gelassen 68
Geld 30, 52, 75, 77, 84, 85, 95, 108
Gelegenheit 5, 70, 86, 96
gelegentlich 81, 82
gelten 84
gemeinsam 28
genießen 44, 72, 77
geplant 30, 73
geradeaus 45, 103
geraten 95, 100, 105
gerissen 29, 67, 100
gesagt, getan 95
geschniegelt und gebügelt 101
Geschmack 58
geschmacklos 62
Geschwätz 25
geschweige denn 71
Gesellschaft 7, 67
Gesicht 13, 25, 41, 46, 74, 88, 95, 96, 101, 110
Gespräch 106
gesund 44, 53, 95, 111
Gewinn 25
Gewissen 26
Gewohnheit 53, 76
gewöhnt 111
Gleich und Gleich 15
Gleichgewicht 108

glimpflich 25, 56
Glück 6, 35, 45, 47, 59, 79
glücklich 46, 81, 112
glücklich und zufrieden 9
Glückskind 17
Gold 15, 70
Gott 26
Gott sei Dank 107
Gotteswillen 95
Gras 15, 37, 67
grausam 9, 63
Grenze 36
griffbereit 10
Grimassen 41
grob gesagt 101
Größe 60, 72
großzügig 45
grün 54, 75
Grund 47, 49
grünes Licht 49
grüßen 75, 84
Gunst 98
günstig 38, 73
gut aussehen 30
gut gelaunt 62
gut stehen 102
Güte 52

H

Haare 10, 39, 40, 42, 53
Hahn 60
Hals 33, 99, 108
Hals über Kopf 57, 82
halten 75, 106, 108
Hand 15, 22, 39, 43, 49, 54, 56, 58, 69, 71, 90, 92, 97, 106, 111
Hände 7, 43, 65, 86, 100, 113
handeln 51
Handumdrehen 63
Hansdampf 64
hart 77, 79, 80
Hase 100, 114
hässlich 111
hastig 61
Häuschen 13
hausen 55
Haut 38, 44
Hehl 17
heimzahlen 26, 40, 49, 84
Heiratsantrag 87
herablassend 106
heranwachsen 53
herausrücken 28
herauswachsen 53
Heringe 83
herumbasteln 78
herumkommandieren 69
herumnörgeln 85
herumreisen 67
herumschnüffeln 80
hervorragend 61
Herz(en) 12, 17, 57, 58, 97, 105
hetzen 97
heutzutage 64
Hilfe 12, 28, 41
Himmel 17, 73, 81
hin und her 11
hin und wieder 40, 80
hinausschreien 116
hineinstehlen 100

121

hineinversetzen 89
Hintergrund 11, 88
hinterherlaufen 104
hinterlassen 70
hinweggehen 84
hinweisen auf 86
hinzu 12
hoch 24
hocharbeiten 115
Hochzeiten 56
Hof machen 31
hoffen 60
Hoffnung(en) 19, 31
höflich 66
Holz 103, 109
Holzweg 104
Honigschlecken 85
hören auf 8
hören 38
Hörner 105
Hühnchen 17, 56
Hund(e) 12, 35, 67, 72, 97, 104
Hundeleben 35, 70
Hut 105

I

ignorieren 75
illegal 111
im Allgemeinen 24, 94
im Bilde sein 67
im Gange 63
im Großen und Ganzen 101
im Nu 64
im Übrigen 21
im Ungewissen 31
immer 10, 28, 45, 52
immer wieder 109

in Anbetracht 73
in flagranti 23
in Ordnung 88, 97
in Reichweite 79
in- und auswendig 67
in voller Länge 46
inkompatibel 62
Innere 110
ins Blaue 99
ins Spiel 19, 86
insgeheim 90

J

Jacke 100
Jahr(e) 93, 116
jammern 101
jetzt oder nie 80
Jubeljahre 17

K

kaltblütig 16, 27, 63
kalte Schulter 27
Kante 88, 90
kaputt 82
kaputtgehen 49, 50, 51, 87
Karriere 6, 47
Karten 69, 70
Kasse 23, 99
Katze 23, 35, 41, 72, 85
Kehrseite 26
Keil 36
Kerl 29, 100
kerngesund 9
Kieker 36
Kind und Kegel 12
Klappe 15, 67

klar 26, 42, 44, 102
klarmachen 19, 26, 36, 60
klassifiziert 111
kleinkriegen 35
Klemme 14, 60
klopfen 109
Klotz 78
klug 54, 57, 58
knapp 21, 56, 99, 100
Knie 94
Knüppel 101
Kohle(n) 55, 90
Kompetenz 50
Kompromiss 12, 103
konfrontiert 41
konfus 10, 62, 100
Kontakt 47, 66, 75
Kontrolle 47, 54, 86
Kopf 24, 39, 55, 56, 57, 59, 67, 72, 79, 88, 89, 90, 97, 110
Kopf und Kragen 93
kosten 115
Kosten 51
kostenlos 24
Kraft 54, 88
Kräfte 65
Kragen 21
Kram 17
krank machen 6
Kriegsbeil 56
Kriegsfuß 31, 81
kritisieren 19, 85
Krone 89
kühl 57, 72
kümmern 74, 78
kurz 99
kurz davor 82, 86
kurzfristig 10, 83, 94
kurzsichtig 9

L

lachen 29
Lachen 69
Ladenschluss 5
Lage 68, 95, 111
lang 71, 74
langatmig 74
Länge 36, 101
langfristig 94, 112
langsam 84
langsam aber sicher 100
langweilen 33
Lärm 54
lässig 45, 81
Last 62
Lauer 112
Lauf 29
Laufenden 67, 75
Laufpass 48, 108
Laune 105
laut 91, 112
Leben 44, 51, 70, 72, 77, 104, 110
leben lassen 73
Lebensunterhalt 18
Leder 10
legen 88, 100
Leiche(n) 32, 71
leichter 96
leichtfertig 111
lesen 91
letzten Endes 95
letztendlich 5, 74
Licht 40, 73, 98, 108
Liebe 75
Lippen 55
loben 16, 25
Loch 68
logisch 55, 102
Lorbeeren 69, 92
losreißen 106
loswerden 47, 48
Luft 6, 26, 59, 72, 112
Luftschlösser 19
Lüge(n) 72, 83
lügen 72
Lust 43, 56
lustig machen 87
Luxus 70

M

Macht 95
mangels 112
mausetot 32
meinen 77, 104
meinetwegen 6
Meinung 6, 14, 24, 34, 50, 78, 87, 101, 112
Menge 33
Menschenverstand 61
Miene 77
Missverständnisse 26
mitgenommen 112
Mitleid 85
mitmachen 8, 57, 71
mitreißen lassen 47
Mittelpunkt 72
mittendrin 14, 107
Mode 23
mögen 75, 84
Mordsspaß 12
Morgenstund 15
Mücke 76
Mühe 11, 22, 83, 109
Mund 15, 60, 65, 77, 99, 109
mündlich 115
Münze 26, 41, 49, 106
Murmeltier 100
Mut 37, 52, 58, 95

N

nach Hause 96
nach und nach 21
nachdenken 22, 24, 89
nachfühlen 43
nachgehen 74, 92, 100
nachjagen 61
nachlassen 34
Nachricht 71, 97
nachschlagen 75
Nächste 24
Nacht 24, 32, 111
Nachteil 30, 81
Nagel 59, 89
Nähe 26, 79
nahe 26, 54
Namen 76, 101
Narr 45
Nase 41, 45, 70, 80, 87
natürlich 29
nebeneinander 99
Neid 52
Nerven 48, 83
nervös 20, 81, 106
Nest 62
neugierig 108
Neuland 18
neulich 32, 82
nicht zuletzt 68
nichts besonders 80, 115
nichts dergleichen 80, 104
Nickerchen 23

Niederlage 41
Niete 36
nörgeln 66
Not 97, 100, 112
Notgroschen 69
Nu 10
Nummer 95
Nuss 80
nützen 52, 96

O

Ochse 37
offensichtlich 8, 26
ohnmächtig 84
Ohr(en) 7, 13, 14, 38, 54, 57, 59, 63, 85, 87, 93
Öl 81
Ölgötzen 37
Ordnung 6, 35, 42, 48, 88
Ort 46

P

Palme 36
Partei ergreifen 84, 99
Party 70
Patsche 64, 101
Pech und Schwefel 10
Pfeife 31
Pferd 22, 89, 114
Pflicht 35
Plage 80
Plan 49, 78, 86, 111
Pläne 70
Platz 49, 116
plötzlich 10, 82
pochen auf 87

prahlen 99
Preis 10
Probe 107, 110
probieren 87
Problem(e) 22, 64, 111
Prüfung 89
pünktlich 9

Q/R

Quere 30
rächen 11, 82, 105
Radau 83

Radieschen 88
Rande 112
rar 63
rastlos 10, 59
Rechnung 24, 45, 61, 109
Recht 65
rechtfertigen 8
Rede(n) 57, 59, 70, 86, 109
Regel 8, 77
Regeln 17, 50, 109
Regen 46, 65, 82
reichlich 40
Reichweite 8
Reihe 73, 102
Reim 57, 89
rein 25, 26, 104
renovieren 35
repräsentieren 102
retten 95
richtige 107
richtig stellen 89
Riemen 48
Risiko 24, 86, 93, 102
Rolle 78

rot 27, 91
Rücken 14, 98, 110
Rückschlag 97
Rücksicht 40, 91
Rückstand 47
Rückzieher 25
Rufweite 53
Ruhe 11, 38, 60, 70, 107
ruhig 9, 66, 72

S

Sache(n) 17, 34, 46, 47, 48, 60, 65, 80, 186, 87, 88, 102, 111
Sackgasse 16
samt und sonders 84
Samthandschuhe 55
Sand 37, 56, 114
schäbig 35
schaden 53
Schade! 86, 98
Schäfchen 42
schaffen 77
scharf 25
Schatten 40, 86, 88, 98, 104
Schein 8
Scheunendrescher 39
schief gehen 8, 50, 62
schimpfen 106
Schippe 92
Schlaf 100
schlafen 32, 100
schlagen 28, 31, 59, 67, 85
schlagfertig 90
schlau 9, 67
schlecht behandeln

schlichten 87
schließen 77, 99
schließlich 5
Schlips 109
Schluss 32, 63
Schlüsse 65
schlüssig sein 55
Schmutz 34
schneiden 29, 30
schnell 9, 21, 30,
 54, 60, 61, 62,
 63, 114, 115
schnell fahren 116
Schnitzer 19
Schnürchen 26
Schock 44
schockiert 90
schöner werden 26
Schraube 57
Schritt 66
Schuld 70, 89
Schule 60, 86
Schwäche 45
schwarz 16, 106
schwarzer Peter 84
schwarzes Schaf 15
schweigen 101, 109
Schweiß 21
Schwierigkeit(en) 10,
 49, 55, 63, 68, 74,
 86, 91, 95, 111, 113
Seele 47
Segel 147
sehen lassen 41
sehnen 74, 116
selbstständig 82
Selbstmord 105
selbstverständlich 8
Semmeln 21, 61, 96
sesshaft werden 97
sicher 7, 9, 23, 63,
 80, 95
Sicherheit 45
Sieg 27
Silber 70
Sinn 40, 104
Sinne(n) 57, 114
sinnvoll 97
sofort 11, 93
sondieren 68
sonnenklar 86
Sonntagskleid 63
Sorge(n) 38, 69
sozusagen 8, 101
sparen 30, 36, 95
Spaß 4, 45, 46, 57, 75
spät 69
Spatz 15, 39, 54
speiübel 9
spendieren 109
Spiel 43, 46, 56,
 77, 86
Spielregeln 46, 93
Spielverderber ??
Spieß 110
Spießruten laufen 47
spontan 81
springlebendig 13
Sprung 31, 87
Sprünge 65
Spur(en) 29, 67
Stand 32
Standpunkt 53
Stärke 87
Staub aufwirbeln 67
Steckenpferd 92
Stegreif 54
stehen bleiben 102
Stein 37
Stelle 102
Stempel 102
sterben 34, 49, 84
Sterne 91
Stich 11, 72, 112
sticheln 85
Stier 105
still 18, 71, 113
stillschweigend 91
Stimme 91, 112
stinksauer 60
Stirn 40, 41, 46
stocktaub 33
stolpern 78
stoßen auf 59
sträuben 55
streben 96
Strecke 19, 61
Strich 5, 7
Stricke 62
Strohhalm 23, 103
Stücke 31, 106
Stühle 100
stundenlang 45
Sturm 103
stürzen 108
Suche 75, 96
suchen 53, 61, 74, 85,
 96, 109
Süßes 57
Szene 16

T

Tacheles 48
Tag 24, 25, 26, 32, 36,
 40, 63, 94
Tageslicht 19
Tassen 14
Tat(en) 77
Tatkraft 48
taub 33, 38, 110
Taube 15, 54
Taugenichts 52
teilhaben 19, 54, 98

teilnehmen 84
Temperatur 90
testen 87
Teufel 37, 101
Teufelskreis 62
Teufelsküche 61
Theater 76
Tiefpunkt 59
Tinte 78
Tisch 24, 25, 70, 104
Tod 23, 33, 95
Todesstoß 67
todmüde 32
töten 19, 31, 35, 105
Tränen 98
traurig 39
treffen 60, 68, 76, 85, 103
trennen 84
Tritt 89
Trockenen 113
Tropfen 37, 68, 103
tropfenweise 37
Trost 7
trotzdem 6, 7
Trüben 113
Tugend 112
typisch 7

U

übel 9, 83
überall 7, 10
übereinstimmen 8, 27, 40, 73
überfahren 94
überfliegen 50
übergeben 108
überhaupt nicht 42
überlassen 71
überlegen 24, 57
Überlegung 81, 96, 108
übermütig 46
übernächste 20, 80
überqueren 27
überrascht 104
überreden 106
überschätzen 47
überschlagen 41
überstürzen 94
übertreiben 69, 85
übertrieben 82
überwinden 19
überzeugen 106
überziehen 100
übrigens 113
Uhr 26, 100
um jeden Preis 29
umkippen 15
umsonst reden 113
Umstände 77, 86
Umweg 94
unbehaglich 38
und Ähnliches 73
unentschlossen 55
Unermessliche 51
unerträglich 14
Unfug 56
ungeschickt 7, 35, 73
ungewiss 6
Ungewissen 31
Unglück 28, 32, 64, 87
Unkenntnis 66
Unklaren 78
Unkraut 62
unmodern 32
Unmögliche 30
unpässlich 111
Unruhe 23
Unschuld 113
unsicher 33, 35
Unsinn 46, 62, 103
untätig 75
unterbrechen 30, 85, 99, 102
Unterfangen 114
unterscheiden 106
unterstützen 102
unverschämt 107
unversehrt 7
unverständlich 9, 26
Unwissenheit 88
unzertrennlich 10
unzuverlässig 44

V

verabschieden 105
verachten 74
verantwortlich 72
Verantwortung 8, 24, 92, 98, 105
verbesserungs-fähig 93
Verbindung 109
verbunden 81
Verderben 28
verdienen 77
vereidigen 104
vererben 54
Verfassung 28, 62
verflixt 31
verfolgen 49, 66
vergessen 13, 80
vergewissern 23
Vergleich 5
Verhältnisse 14, 73
verkehren 55, 66
verlassen 39, 58, 112
verlegen 61
verletzen 30, 90
verlieben 57, 75

verlieren 29, 44, 58, 75, 107, 108
Verlust(e) 80, 86, 96
vermitteln 89
Vermutung 99, 114
vernachlässigbar 25
vernachlässigen 72
Vernunft 60, 112
vernünftig 36, 97
verraten 49, 72, 101, 106
verrückt 9, 14, 36, 50, 51, 76, 80
verschließen 26, 99
verschonen 72
verschuldet 63
verschwinden 34, 100
Versenkung 100
Versprechen 50
Versprecher 100
verstehen 52, 78, 97, 107
Versuch 50, 99, 110
versuchen 50, 5, 6, 110
verteilen 98
vertreten 102, 103
verunglücken 4, 78
verursachen 49
verwechseln 106
verwenden 111
verzählen 29
verzetteln 57
verzweifeln 34
Verzweiflung 36, 116
viel mehr 95
Vogel 2, 73
Vogelperspektive 112
Vollbremsung 64
Volldampf 7
vollenden 94
volljährig 6

von oben herab 61
von vorn 110
vorankommen 47, 77, 87
Vorbehalt 104
vorbeikommen 37, 87
vorbeischauen 21, 37, 103
vordrängeln 65
Vorfahrt 116
vorgeben 84
vorletzte 68
Vorliebe 94, 105
vornehm tun 6
vorschlagen 28
vorsichtig 51, 55
Vorteil 5, 30, 110

W

Waage 12
Wahnsinn 112
wahnsinnig 36, 76, 78
wappnen 8
warnen 89
warten 55, 59, 72, 100, 112
Wasser 22, 33, 44, 57, 66, 113
wecken 35, 67, 72
Weg 73, 77, 85, 113, 114
wegkommen 47
weinen 30, 52
Weisheit 10
weitergeben 54, 84
weiterhin 66, 88
weitermachen 22
weiterwursteln 65
weitgehend 84

Welt(en) 13, 29, 49, 72, 81, 102
wer A ... sagt 63
Wert 103
Wesentliche 87
Wespennest 60
Wettlauf 5, 90, 109
wettmachen 76
wichtig 22
Wichtigkeit 68
Widerrede 20
widersetzen 102
widersprechen 8
Widerspruch 7, 28, 94
Widerstand 73
widerwillig 92
wild wachsen 114
Wille(n) 113, 114
willkommen 61, 99
wimmeln 6
Wind 16, 114
Wink 59
Witz 29
Woche 32
Wolf 98
Wort(e) 39, 50, 69, 88, 105, 114, 115
Wort brechen 11
Wörtchen 57
Wunder 99, 115
wunder Punkt 87
wünschen 70, 97
Wurzel 103, 106
Wut 16, 44, 51, 56, 107
wütend 9, 61, 75, 106

Z

zäh 10
zählen 19

127

Zähne 12, 52
Zankapfel 17
zanken 42
Zaunpfahl 59
Zeilen 14, 37, 91
Zeit 5, 6, 29, 32, 37, 38, 43, 58, 64, 67, 69, 71, 72, 74, 77, 84, 86, 90, 94, 105, 108, 109, 110, 112, 113
Zeitvertreib 92
zerstört 52
Zeug 30
ziehen 34, 105
ziellos 10
zieren 6
Zivilcourage 57
Zorn 40, 41
zu allererst 86

zu etwas bringen 28
zu sich kommen 28
zu zweit gehen 83
zuerst 10
Zufall 73
zufällig 4, 21, 24, 27, 55
zufällig begegnen 94
zufrieden geben 97
Zug 78
Zügel 92
zügeln 66, 92
zuhören 84
zukommen lassen 106
Zukunft 51, 74
zumuten 15
zunächst 12, 43, 45, 102
Zunge 57, 75
Zungenspitze 109

Zünglein 12
zur Sache 28
zurechtkommen 43
zurücklehnen 97
zurückzahlen 84
zusammenbrechen 18, 51
zusammenhalten 102
zusammenreißen 88
zusammenzucken 102
zu Schulden 16
zuspitzen 28
zustande bringen 19
zutreffen 110
Zutritt 81
zwanglos 38
Zweck 8, 97, 111
zwecklos 40
Zweifel 57, 80
Zwischenstation 103